PHILLIPS BROOKS

CAUSES AND THEIR CHAMPIONS

BY

M. A. DeWOLFE HOWE

AN · ATLANTIC · MONTHLY · PRESS · PUBLICATION

Illustrated

BOSTON
LITTLE, BROWN, AND COMPANY
1926

THE ATLANTIC MONTHLY PRESS PUBLICATIONS
ARE PUBLISHED BY
LITTLE, BROWN, AND COMPANY
IN ASSOCIATION WITH
THE ATLANTIC MONTHLY COMPANY

PRINTED IN THE UNITED STATES OF AMERICA

PREFACE

THE wiseacres in the field of books are fond of saying that there is a great deal in the choice of a title. Doubtless they are right, and possibly some of them, if they happen to read this book, will be disposed to say that the unity of its theme would be more apparent had it been called "Studies in American Idealism." Those words, indeed, would have defined it, but somewhat more vaguely than the title that has been adopted. "Causes and Their Champions," as a descriptive phrase, may possess the advantage that it suggests with some definiteness the double purpose of this book: to deal in turn with a series of causes — movements, reforms, call them what you will — directly affecting contemporary life in America; and to present each one of them in special relation to the life and work of the man or woman — the champion — most clearly identified with its furtherance. The cause of anti-slavery, with Garrison as champion, is omitted only as a *res adjudicata*.

Here, then, against a background of reform in various directions a series of biographical studies is offered. History and biography are mingled, after no set formula, but in the hope that each will add something to the vitality and value of the other. To bring the treatment of each topic within the reasonable compass of a single chapter much selection and elimination have been required. The sources to which these methods have been applied may be scanned by the curious and the ambitious in the lists at the further end of the volume. If after considering the whole matter a reader wishes to inscribe on the title-page the subtitle, "Studies in American Idealism," there will be no protest from the author.

He does not deceive himself with the belief that "come-outers" and their idealistic pursuits are held in any special favor at the present moment. There is indeed a popular opinion to the effect that if the reformers of the past century had let things alone we should have been better off in many ways. But this is merely an "if of history." The counter-if of a civilization without causes or champions would provide the speculative with quite as much food for thought.

It is impossible to enumerate the many persons whose counsel at one point and another has been sought and gratefully followed in the preparation of this volume. It is equally impossible to omit a special word of gratitude for constant helpfulness from the Librarian and staff of that blessed focus of teeming shelves and quiet alcoves, the Boston Athenæum.

M. A. DeW. H.

Boston
May, 1926

CONTENTS

ILLUSTRATIONS

CAUSES AND THEIR CHAMPIONS

I

THE RED CROSS AND CLARA BARTON

It is a glaring truism that not a single movement for the amelioration of human existence, not a single "cause" or "reform," has reached the point of accomplishing anything without a sacrificial effort on the part of one man or woman. Before the final achievement scores or hundreds more will have made their contribution to it. But almost invariably it is possible to look back, when the ends are accomplished, and to single out the person most closely identified with their beginnings. Here the cause to be considered is what the founders of the American Red Cross called "the progress of mercy," through the organization of that national spirit of philanthropy which, without undue self-gratulation, may be regarded as an American characteristic. With the establishment of this cause, and with its promotion to the stage from which the American Red Cross was developed into the vast agency for good which it proved itself in the World War, the name of Clara Barton must always be linked. Cause and champion have seldom been more closely identified.

Clara Barton lived for more than ninety years, much beset with physical weakness through more than the first half of them, yet manifesting before the age of fifty such powers of physical endurance as the strongest man might envy. While she was still in her early forties, the Red Cross had its origin in Switzerland. A few years later — during the Franco-Prussian War — it became intimately known to her, and she took part in its operations at the battle front. Thus the person and the cause came into definite contact. To look first at the one by herself, then at the other by itself, and finally at the two in conjunction, is to discover afresh what can be brought to pass by the sustained, whole-hearted devotion of individual powers to a great object. It is also to recognize the place of a strong personal link between origins and results.

I

When Clara Barton was born in a farmhouse at Oxford, Worcester County, Massachusetts, on Christmas Day, 1821, Samuel Richardson's novel, *Clarissa Harlowe*, made up of eight volumes of correspondence in the vein of eighteenth-century romance, was less secure as a classic than it is to-day; but, perhaps for that very reason, it meant more to its readers. It meant so much to Stephen Barton and his wife, Sarah (Stone) Barton — or at least to one of them — that the youngest of their five children, younger by ten years than her next older sister, received the name of Clarissa Harlowe Barton. The "Clarissa" was soon abridged into Clara. The "Harlowe" survived, at least until 1867, when "Clara Harlowe Barton" was the subject of a memoir in L. P. Brockett's *Women in the Civil War*, a volume adorned with an engraved frontispiece designated "Miss Clara H. Barton."

The simple name of Clara Barton was much more suited to her as both girl and woman. Her early background was simplicity itself. Her father was a substantial farmer, of sound New England stock, who had fought under "Mad Anthony" Wayne. His interest in military and political matters never left him, and at his knee his youngest daughter acquired an early knowledge of army and government affairs. "I thought the President," she wrote in later years, "might be as large as the meeting-house, and the Vice-President perhaps the size of the schoolhouse." At the same time she gained the understanding which enabled her to declare of herself in war-time: "I never addressed a colonel as captain, got my cavalry on foot, or mounted my infantry!" In her father also she had an early instructor in the value of the philanthropic interests which were included in his spirit of patriotism. Her mother, a notable New England housewife, was a woman of strong will and a quick temper.

From such parents an inheritance of fear was something abnormal; yet, in looking back on her own childhood, Clara Barton once wrote, "I remember nothing but fear." When she was sent away from home to school as a little girl her timidity at table kept her from eating the food set before her, and it was found necessary to return her to her parents. Their liberality of spirit made them Universalists and "come-outers" in general, afraid not even of phrenologists, one of whom, consulted with regard to the timorous Clara, pronounced: "The sensitive nature will always remain. She will never assert herself for herself; she will suffer wrong first. But for others she will be perfectly fearless. Throw responsibility upon her."

This prescription was fulfilled largely by the force of circumstances. For one thing, in the words of an account of her work in the Civil War, "she was early taught that primal benediction, miscalled a curse, which requires mankind to earn their bread." Like her parents, her older brothers and sisters were workers. Activity of body and mind

CLARA BARTON, 1867

charged the atmosphere in which she grew up.
Besides learning early to cook and to wash — em-
ployments to which she often turned in her later
years — she was taught to paint a house, to weave
at a hand loom, to make herself a straw hat from
blades of rye of her own cutting and bleaching. In
ways of greater daring her brother David, whom
she greatly admired and afterwards described as
"the Buffalo Bill of the surrounding country,"
taught her much. When she was no more than five
years old he used to take her to a field in which
their father's blooded colts were pastured, seize
and bridle two of them, and — to quote Clara Barton's own words — "gathering the reins of both
bridles firmly in hand, throw me upon the back of
one colt, spring upon the other himself, and catch-
ing me by one foot, and bidding me 'cling fast to
the mane,' gallop away over field and fen, in and
out among the other colts in wild glee like ourselves." From that, her only riding-school, she acquired a horsemanship which in war-time stood her
in good stead.

Through the same teacher came her first experience of nursing. When she was about ten years old
this paragon of older brothers suffered serious injuries in falling from a ridgepole at a barn-raising.
For two years, until she was twelve and he had

recovered, she made herself his assiduous nurse. Her schooling was completely interrupted and she hardly left the invalid's room. Her own health suffered, she ceased to grow, — her stature remaining but little more than five feet, — but the experience left her highly skilled in the care of the sick.

She appears in general to have led a model childhood, conquering her timidities, accepting meekly her parents' refusal to let her learn dancing, and acquitting herself creditably at the schools of her native town, where she was taught in part by her sisters and brother Stephen, and became a teacher herself. This seemed her destined employment, as it seemed, but was not, theirs. After eighteen years of it in and about Oxford, she felt the need of a more thorough mental training and went in 1852 — as later young women of her type would have sought a college — to the Liberal Institute at Clinton, New York, from which she emerged a year later, at thirty-two, a well-equipped "Yankee schoolmarm."

A "teacher dyed in the wool" was what she called herself at this period. Somewhat fortuitously she drifted from Massachusetts, via Clinton, New York, to Bordentown, New Jersey, where, with the true spirit of a pioneer, she volunteered and was permitted to conduct the first public school in the place. A strong local sentiment opposed the opening of such a "pauper school," but Clara Barton, beginning with six pupils in 1853, gave over in 1855 to a male principal the charge of six hundred pupils — her biographers assure us — assembled in the building she had led the town to erect. For this success she paid dear through a breakdown involving the complete loss of her voice. To recuperate she moved to Washington, unaware that her school-teaching was over and that for nearly sixty years she was to live chiefly at the national capital, in a close relation, through many of these years, with the government and its administrators.

Here again she became a sort of pioneer, as one of the first, if not the very first, of women employed as a government clerk on the same terms with men. It was not an easy berth which she found in the Patent Office at $1400 a year. The male clerks, among whom there was plenty of incompetence and dishonesty, resented her presence, puffed tobacco smoke in her face, and made her generally uncomfortable. Her "copperplate" handwriting, her faithfulness and complete integrity, did not save her from dismissal in 1857, when, in the Buchanan administration, she fell under the ban of Black Republicanism. She had heard Sumner's speech,

"The Crime against Kansas," the night before he was assaulted in the Senate, and long afterwards declared that the Civil War began "not at Sumter but at Sumner." Dismissed from her post in 1857, she spent nearly two years with her family in Oxford until recalled to straighten out the Patent Office records entangled by her absence.

So she found herself at forty a useful servant of the government at Washington, a small woman, of simple habit, with brown eyes and brown hair, — in which she said much later that one gray hair was to be found, though she had forgotten just where, — with a soft voice that grew deep instead of shrill under stress of the anger of which she was healthily capable, with pronounced, regular, and mobile features, neither beautiful nor the reverse. Unlike Florence Nightingale, the great Crimean prototype of war nurses, — a personage of whom Clara Barton had hardly heard as late as 1863 when somebody called her "the Florence Nightingale of America," — she was without the advantages, serviceable even in America, of a commanding social position. This lever for reform was hardly required in the highly personal work which she undertook in the Civil War. It did not call for any great arraying of forces and influences behind her. Her kinsman and biographer, the Rev. William E. Barton, makes a significant statement in saying: "She was never able to look upon armies as mere masses of troops; she had to remember that they were individual men, each capable of suffering pain in his own person, and each of them carrying with him to the front the anxious thoughts of loved ones at home."

The very first instance of Clara Barton's helpfulness to Union soldiers was typical of its intensely personal character throughout the war. The Sixth Massachusetts Regiment, from which the first blood of the war was drawn as it passed through Baltimore, reached Washington late in April 1861, and, in the general dearth of accommodations, was quartered in the United States Senate Chamber. Here Miss Barton visited the soldiers, found friends and acquaintances from Worcester among them, and, establishing herself in the Speaker's chair, read aloud to them from a recent copy of the *Worcester Spy* which had somehow followed them to Washington. To that journal she immediately sent advertisements declaring that she would distribute personally any supplies or money sent to her for wounded and needy members of the regiment. The response was such that she was obliged to secure space in a Washington warehouse. This was the method she continued to practise. Her own modest competence, supplemented by the Patent Office salary, which an honorable arrangement with superiors and fellow workers enabled her to go on drawing, provided her with funds which she devoted generously to the cause she was asking others to further. At every turn her work was direct and immediate.

All this while the United States Sanitary Commission and, in lesser degree, the Christian Commission were organizing and developing work much more like that of the Red Cross in later years than anything Clara Barton was doing. Towards the end of the war Clara Barton accepted an appointment as "Superintendent of the Department of Nurses for the Army of the James"; but for the most part she was essentially a free lance, whose view of her own status was frankly that of the individualist, — indeed the egotist, — to be found in every pioneer and reformer. "If I have by practice," she wrote in 1864, "acquired any skill, it belongs to me to use untrammeled, and I might not work as efficiently, or labor as happily, under the direction of those of less experience than myself."

This experience of hers was indeed extensive. It began and for the better part of the first war-year was concentrated in Washington where she ministered to wounded soldiers as they returned from the battle front and in the hospitals. In the spring of

1862 she was called for several months to her old home in Oxford, Massachusetts, by the illness and death of her father. That old soldier encouraged her impulse to "follow the cannon," not to wait for wounded soldiers to be brought from the front, but to go to the front herself and care for them there. When her father died, in March 1862, she proceeded at once to deal with the red tape which impeded the execution of any such strange purpose in any unattached woman. Her own inhibitions had already been conquered. "I struggled long and hard," she afterwards wrote, "with my sense of propriety — with the appalling fact that I was a woman whispering in one ear, and thundering in the other the groans of suffering men dying like dogs, unfed and unsheltered, for the life of every institution which had protected and educated me! I said that I struggled with my sense of propriety, and I say it with humiliation and shame. I am ashamed that I thought of such a thing." It was not till July and August 1862 that the coveted passes to the front were actually issued.

The extraordinary uses to which she put the opportunities thus opened to her form the subjects of successive chapters in her biographies. Here they can only be suggested. From Cedar Mountain, in August 1862, through Fredericksburg at the end of the year, she served at the very front in such historic fights as Chantilly, Harper's Ferry, South Mountain, and Antietam.   At one place she found herself in care of a young man who had carried her satchel as a schoolboy; at another, of the sexton of her home church in Oxford. At Antietam a soldier standing beside her was shot dead. At Fredericksburg she crossed the Rappahannock on the pontoon bridge with troops under Confederate fire. Everywhere she was winning her title of "the angel of the battlefield" — ministering to the wounded, spent, and dying, making and distributing gruel or crackers stirred into a mixture of wine, whiskey, and water, sweetened with coarse brown sugar, even yielding to a soldier's entreaties to use her own penknife to remove a bullet from his cheek. After Fredericksburg and a fresh assembling of supplies in Washington, she passed eight months of 1863 with the troops besieging Charleston, came as near as a noncombatant could to taking part in the assault on Fort Wagner, and nursed the very Negroes who were to thank her thirty years later when she was administering Red Cross relief after the Sea Islands hurricane.

"Not an ordinary nurse, but a sort of independent sanitary commission" — so she permitted herself to be defined in later years. Still in that capacity

she reached the front after the Wilderness and Spott-
sylvania, and, finding the hospital conditions unspeakably bad, made a flying return to Washington,
described the true state of affairs to her friend Senator (subsequently Vice-President) Henry Wilson of
Massachusetts, after nightfall, with the result that
at two o'clock the next morning the Quartermaster
General and his staff were on the way to Fredericksburg, and by noon of that day the neglected men
were receiving proper care. Similarly effective,
though achieved through more regular channels, was
her work as Superintendent of Nurses, under General
B. F. Butler, for most of the remainder of the war.
When it was over, one of her most valuable pieces
of war-work was still to be done — a task truly
foreshadowing one of the great achievements of the
Red Cross in the World War. This was the search for
missing men. A long and romantic story — especially with respect to the graves of the prisoners
who died at Andersonville — might be told about
it. The results were of such notable value that
Congress liberally reimbursed Clara Barton for
the drain it had made upon her own purse and
effort.

For the lavish expenditure of her strength
through all these years there could be no requital —
only a penalty, which came, as it had come at the

end of her teaching, in the form of the complete failure of her voice, occurring this time when, in 1868, she stood in a crowded auditorium, opened her mouth to speak, and produced no sound whatever. For the nervous prostration of which this was the signal, her physician ordered the rest to be found only in Europe, where the Red Cross, all unknown to her, was in its early infancy.

To Europe she went in 1869, no longer the child of fears, but the woman of energy and resource, tried and skilled in the relief of human suffering, broken for the time by the excessive use of her own great strength.

II

It is the fashion of writers about the origin of the International Red Cross — and there have been many of them — to point for ancient examples of mercy to the Crusades, from which the Knights of St. John of Jerusalem, the supporters of the St. John's Ambulance Association in England, trace their descent, and even to the Good Samaritan, the very pattern of a Red Cross worker. In pre-Christian times the records of kindness between hostile nationals are far to seek. For the time between the Crusades and our own day, Miss Mabel T. Boardman, in her book, *Under the Red Cross Flag*, cites a significant instance of the merciful treatment of wounded men recorded by Ambroise Paré in his account of the Campaign of Turin in 1537:

Being come into the city I entered into a stable thinking to lodge my own and my man's horse and found four dead soldiers and three propped against the wall, their features all changed and they neither saw, heard, nor spake, and their clothes were still smoldering where the gunpowder had burnt them. As I was looking at them with pity there came an old soldier who asked me if there were any way to cure them. I said "No." And then he went up to them and cut their throats very gently, and without ill will toward them. Seeing this great cruelty, I told him he was a villain; he answered that he prayed God when he should be in such a plight he might find someone to do the same for him that he should not linger in misery.

It was indeed all a pretty grim story until Florence Nightingale went to the Crimean War in 1854, established her system of nursing at Scutari, and opened the eyes of England and all the civilized world to what might be but never previously had been.

The broad extension of measures for relieving the misery of battles might have remained in the realm of imagination had not a Swiss, Henry Dunant, thirty-one years old in 1859, happened to be traveling in northern Italy at the time and to see for himself the hideous sufferings that followed the battle of Solferino, at which the Austrians were defeated by allied armies of Italy and France. The medical

corps of an army was then without any treaty protection, and naturally remained with its own troops,
whether pursued or pursuing. The wounded, tram-
pled under foot and left in the rear, could only fare
as best they might. Dunant encountered them in
agonies in villages near the battle front, neglected,
dying, submitting to unskillful operations without
anæsthetics. A citizen of a neutral country, he organized a volunteer corps of Italian women, and
with their help did what he could to mitigate the
pains of Italian, French, and Austrian alike, observing in suffering no dividing lines of nationality.
What is more, he made his experience the subject of
a pamphlet, *Un Souvenir de Solferino* (1862), which
presented his story of an eyewitness in ghastly
detail, and, in justification for so doing, asked:
"Would it not be possible to found and organize in
all civilized countries permanent societies of volun-
teers which in time of war would render succor to
the wounded *without distinction of nationality?*"

The pamphlet, translated into various languages,
attracted a vast amount of attention throughout
Europe, not only in the general public, but among
the responsible rulers. In his native city of Geneva
there was, by good fortune, an organization, the
Société Genevoise d'Utilité Publique, which had
for its very object the promotion of humanitarian

UN SOUVENIR

DE

SOLFERINO

PAR

J. HENRY DUNANT

Troisième Edition

GENÈVE
IMPRIMERIE DE JULES-Gᵐᵉ FICK
—
1863

TITLE-PAGE OF THE BOOK WHICH BROUGHT
THE RED CROSS INTO BEING

causes. In Henry Dunant's suggestion the Society saw a possibility of public service, and brought together at Geneva, in October of 1863, representatives of fourteen nations to discuss the draft of an agreement designed to attain the end in view. The discussion was so promising that the Swiss Government took the matter in hand, and invited twenty-five sovereign states to send delegates to a diplomatic convention to be held at Geneva in August 1864.

The great result of this meeting was the adoption of the Convention of Geneva, an international agreement "For the Amelioration of the Condition of the Wounded in Armies at the Field." Within a year fifteen nations — including France, Great Britain, Prussia, and other German states — had ratified it; before the Franco-Prussian War in 1870 there were twenty-two adherents to the treaty. Modified and extended by later international conferences, especially through the inclusion of naval as well as military provisions, the original Convention marked a great forward step by rendering neutral and immune from injury in war the sick and wounded and all who cared for them. Though it did not employ the term "Red Cross" to designate its object, the seventh article of the Convention read: "A distinctive and uniform flag shall be adopted for hospitals, ambulances, and evacuations. It must on every occasion be accompanied by the national flag. An arm-badge (brassard) shall also be allowed for individuals neutralized, but the delivery thereof shall be left to military authority. The flag and the arm-badge shall bear a red cross on a white ground." This emblem, reversing the white cross on the red field of the Swiss national banner, was adopted in compliment to the government of neutral Switzerland, which had issued the summons for the conference. The delegates were probably unaware that after the Crimean War Queen Victoria had presented Florence Nightingale with a diamond brooch, designed by the versatile Prince Consort, bearing the royal cypher and a St. George's cross in red enamel, all within an encircling inscription, "Blessed Are the Merciful."

How was the United States represented at the establishment of the Red Cross? Only by informal delegates. This could hardly have been otherwise when the government had a civil war of its own on its hands. Our Minister to Switzerland, George C. Fogg, and the European agent of the Sanitary Commission, Charles S. P. Bowles, were indeed authorized by the Secretary of State, William H. Seward, "to attend the meeting in an informal manner, for the purpose of giving or receiving such suggestions as you may think likely to promote the humane ends which have prompted it." In diplomatic language he proceeded to caution them against attending the conference if the Southern Confederacy was to be represented in it. The wariness of "entangling alliances," on which more recent years have laid a familiar emphasis, called forth the statement, credited to Secretary Seward: "Our government, while always ready to forward all humanitarian action, has a well-understood policy of holding itself aloof from all European congresses and compacts of a political nature. . . . The government wishes to act as a free agent, with option in the premises, and in its own good time." Evidently the project fired our authorities with no enthusiasm. Even the sage Lincoln is reported to have looked upon it as "a fifth wheel to the military coach."

Yet Fogg and Bowles did attend the congress, and Bowles, armed with photographs and abundant information concerning the beneficent work which the Sanitary Commission was doing in the United States at that very moment, made an effective contribution to the conclusions at which the delegates arrived. Even so, the most complacent American might well have been excused for rubbing his eyes when he read in a letter written at the beginning of the Spanish War by the Secretary of State,

William R. Day, to the Secretary of War, defining the national and international status of the American Red Cross, these words: "It is to be remembered that the Geneva Convention itself is largely the outgrowth of American initiative." In the course of a single human generation strange myths may assume the respectability of apparent truth.

III

When Clara Barton went to Europe in 1869, she chanced to settle in Geneva. If the Red Cross organization was unknown to her, she herself was by no means unknown to the gentlemen of Geneva who constituted its central committee, M. Gustave Moynier, its president, Dr. Louis Appia, and others, for a resounding fame of her work in our Civil War had reached Europe before her. When these officials called upon her, as they promptly did, it was to ask why the United States, after five years, was still holding aloof from the Geneva Convention, and what could be done about it. Clara Barton had to confess that she was quite ignorant of the Red Cross plan — an ignorance the more surprising since the Rev. Dr. Henry W. Bellows, head of the U. S. Sanitary Commission, had, only the year before, visited a second International Red Cross Conference in Paris and, on his return to America, had renewed, without any success, the attempt he had previously made to interest the United States government in the enterprise.

What Miss Barton's Genevan visitors told her of their work made a strong impression upon her. She proceeded to inform herself more fully about it, and within a year found herself faced with an opportunity to acquire a knowledge of the Red Cross, not merely in theory but in practice. In July 1870 the Franco-Prussian War broke upon a startled Europe. Clara Barton, still invalid, was living in a villa at Berne. Here, within a few days of the declaration of war, she was amazed to receive a visit from the Grand Duchess of Baden, the only daughter of King Wilhelm of Prussia, soon to become Emperor Wilhelm I of Germany. This royal personage, a devoted supporter of the Red Cross movement, between whom and Clara Barton a relation of sympathetic friendship soon came to exist, sought her aid — as that of one whose fame gave assurance that it was well worth seeking — in the organization of such relief as the impending war was sure to demand. A few days later the Swiss officials of the International Red Cross, on their way to the seat of war, called upon her with a similar request. She pleaded her invalid condition, but could not bring herself to say No, and within a

week was following them to Basle. "As I journeyed on," she wrote at a later day, "and saw the work of these Red Cross societies in the field, accomplishing in four months under their systematic organization what we failed to accomplish in four years without it, — no mistakes, no needless suffering, no starving, no lack of care, no waste, no confusion, but order, plenty, cleanliness, and comfort wherever that little flag made its way, a whole continent marshaled under the banner of the Red Cross, — as I saw all this, and joined and worked in it, you will not wonder that I said to myself, 'If I live to return to my country I will try to make my people understand the Red Cross and that treaty.' " The cause and its champion had at last come completely together.

It is for a biography rather than for such a separate paper as this to follow Clara Barton through the Franco-Prussian War. She will be found at many vital points of its progress — as at Sedan, after its fall, ministering to the wounded; entering Strassburg with the German army, and, in pursuance of the principle of modern charity, organizing a workroom in which for eight months poor women made articles of clothing at the rate of fifteen hundred garments a week, at once meeting an immediate need and preserving their own self-respect as wage-earners; at the siege of Paris, which she entered, as she had entered Sedan, with the German troops. There she administered relief on the fall of the city, and, a few months later, during the Commune. Her letters through all this time make no secret of the fact that the French, as she saw them, were distasteful to her. Under her Yankee scrutiny they appeared "dirty but fashionable," and so doubly offensive. "It is a real merit in me," she wrote, "to work for the French. I do it out of pity and charity towards suffering humanity — because they needed it and not because I gratify my love or my taste by it." In the autumn of 1871 she carried this Red Cross principle to the relief of distress in northern France, and celebrated Christmas with a famous party for her workwomen in Strassburg. Through all this time, she was cementing her friendship with the Grand Duchess of Baden and other ardent believers in the Red Cross.

"As thy days, so shall thy strength be." The truth of this assurance was well illustrated by Clara Barton's amazing first experience of Europe. Through the war her invalidism disappeared. When it was over she collapsed. Travel and a winter in London — where she would have seen Florence Nightingale had they not both been ill — accomplished little or nothing for her recovery. At times all her letter-writing had to be done with bandaged eyes. To nervous prostration definite troubles with throat and chest were added. Early in October 1873, she sailed for home, pitiably poor in strength, immensely richer in experience for her four years abroad, and eager to turn to such account as her powers would permit the fruits of it all. On the steamer that brought her home she indulged her propensity to write verses, of slender merit as such. They were called "Have Ye Room?" and were read to her fellow passengers at the usual "concert." The seriousness with which she took the mission of her return, with a clear trace of the forgivable egotism of a sick woman conscious of great things done and still to be done, found summary expression in the final couplet:

Have ye place, each beloved one, a place in your prayer,
Have ye *room*, my dear countrymen, room for me there?

IV

The episode of Red Cross history with which the life of Clara Barton was now to be interwoven may well be read with a special attention on the part of Americans in sympathy — and indeed out of sympathy — with the general purposes of the League of Nations as an agency for the promotion of better international relations. On a more limited scale such was the object of the Convention of Geneva. It took eighteen years — from 1864 to 1882 — to secure the adhesion of the United States to this agreement, to overcome the identical objections that have been urged against American participation in the work of the League. It was through the persistent, intelligent effort of one woman, Clara Barton, that the United States was finally brought to join with the other civilized nations of the world in a task of international helpfulness long regarded as fraught with danger.

For nearly four years after Clara Barton's return from Europe in 1873 she could do little but seek the restoration of her health. She found it at Dansville, New York, where she lived for most of this time, first in a sanitarium, then in a house of her own. By 1877, when the Russo-Turkish War was threatening Europe with another upheaval, she was enough better to enter into correspondence with the Red Cross officials in Geneva about making a fresh effort to enlist the government and people of the United States in the organized relief which might soon be sorely needed. Dr. Bellows, disheartened by his two failures to accomplish anything, advised her "to give it up as hopeless"; yet, recognizing the "never-say-die" spirit in which she continued to face the adventure, wrote to her when it was nearing its successful issue: "I trust you will press this matter upon our present administration with all the weight of your well-earned influence. Having myself somewhat ignominiously failed to get any encouragement for this measure from two administrations, I leave it in your more fortunate hands, hoping that the time is ripe for a less jealous policy than American self-isolation in international movements for extending and universalizing mercy towards the victims of war."

Into her "more fortunate hands" came also a letter from her Genevan friend, M. Moynier, president of the International Committee of the Red Cross, addressed to the President of the United States, appealing yet again for American adherence to the Convention of Geneva. With this communication Miss Barton betook herself again to Washington, but, before presenting it to President Hayes, sought to strengthen her cause by explaining it to influential members of the government in Congress and the State and War Departments. Their ignorance and apathy were hard to conquer. She had found besides, on inquiry at the State Department, that the record against the proposal, "on the ground of danger from *entangling alliances*," — the italics are hers, — still stood in its way. Yet she secured an interview with President Hayes, who received her and

M. Moynier's letter with respect — and referred it to his Secretary of State, Hamilton Fish. Nothing happened; the earlier negatives to the Geneva proposal seemed beyond reversal; and, like a wise woman, Clara Barton decided to await the change of heart which a change of administration might bring about.

In President Garfield she had a friend, with the bond of common experience in war itself. To him, soon after he took office, she presented the letters from M. Moynier which had so little moved the previous administration. Both he and his Secretary of State, James G. Blaine, to whom it was referred, received it most hospitably. Blaine gave his careful attention to Miss Barton's exposition of her cause, deplored its previous failures, declaring that "the Monroe doctrine was not made to ward off humanity," and dismissed her rejoicing in the reasonable hope that something would be done, and promptly. So, doubtless, it would have been, but for Garfield's assassination.

The delay that ensued, grievous as it was, had its compensations. Clara Barton had shown her resource in meeting one objection to an American Red Cross organization — namely, that the United States was not a nation for which war was to be expected — by proposing that here, in times of peace, the Red Cross should stand ready to give aid in national calamities: a provision, by the way, which was later made, and was adopted by the International Red Cross as the "American Amendment." Encouraged, moreover, by President Garfield, she had organized at Washington just before his death, and nearly a year before the Red Cross treaty was ratified, an association incorporated as "The American Association of the Red Cross." When she went to Dansville for the summer, her friends and neighbors there organized (August 22, 1881), in compliment to her, the first local Red Cross Society in the United States. Almost immediately the news of disastrous forest fires in Michigan gave the infant society an opportunity for usefulness. In the neighboring cities of Rochester and Syracuse, benevolent men and women lent their aid to the work begun in Dansville. Money and supplies in liberal quantities were forwarded to the Michigan sufferers until the relief committee of that state sent word that no more help was needed. Apart from standing as the first instance of Red Cross relief in America, this piece of prompt, effective work became a telling point of evidence in favor of the American Red Cross as Clara Barton was pleading for it.

For pleading was still necessary. In the autumn

of 1881 Clara Barton returned to Washington, where she found President Arthur, whom she visited at once, as well disposed towards the Red Cross project as Garfield had been. Among other officials of the government there was little or no active opposition — with a corresponding absence of enthusiasm. It was evident that without a determined prodding of government and people nothing could be accomplished. Before the end of 1881 Miss Barton issued an Address to the President, Congress, and People of the United States, expanding a stillborn pamphlet which she had produced three years before, and pleading passionately for the object nearest to her heart. Its vein is marked in these sentences: "My first and greatest endeavor has been to wipe from the scroll of my country's fame the stain of imputed lack of common humanity, to take her out of the roll of barbarism. I said that in 1869 there were twenty-two nations in the compact. There are now thirty-one, for since that date have been added Roumania, Persia, San Salvador, Servia, Bolivia, Chili, Argentine Republic, and Peru. If the United States of America is fortunate and diligent, she may, perhaps, come to stand No. 32 in roll of civilization and humanity. If not, she will remain where she at present stands, among the barbarians and the heathen."

The tide had turned, though she seemed hardly aware of the fact. One evidence of it was that rival societies, to her excessive irritation, were springing into being. She felt that powerful influences were opposing her, and, true to her kinsman-biographer's definition of her as "normally responsive to praise and abnormally sensitive to criticism," wrote in her diary one day: "All the society people of the city and country seem to be arrayed in arms against me, with only my single hand, sore heart, and silent tongue to make my way against misrepresentation, malice, and selfish ambition." In reality her tongue was no more silent than her pen, which she took in hand, less than a month before her fight was won, to write to Frances Willard, in terms concretely foreshadowing the later struggle over the League of Nations:

It is hard and heavy and bitter; the shots of malice and de-traction fall thick, but I must stand at the helm and steer my ship safely into port. The *Treaty of Geneva* must first be secured. I have but one passage to take it through and that is lined thick on every side with guns manned by the society ladies of the Capitol of the Nation. The Red Cross, a little stranger craft from foreign lands, bearing only the banner of peace and love, and her messages of world-wide mercy begging shelter and acceptance in our capacious harbour, has chosen me for her pilot to bring her in. Besides these guns that open upon her from all sides she runs against the chains which have so long held her out — fancied Government defenses of "Non-intervention," "Self-isolation," beware of "Entangling alliances," "Washington's Farewell Address," "Monroe Doctrine," apathy, inertia, general ignorance, national conceit, national distrust, a desire to retain the old-time barbarous privileges of privateering and piracy which we have hugged as a precious boon against every humane treaty since we began. . . . Never a messenger of mercy met a more inhospitable welcome, but the poor battered pilot has faith in the craft, and faith in God, and at no distant day, in spite of all, we shall throw out a sturdy old iron anchor to grapple with the reefs of the coast, and run up a little pennant beside the cross, "Treaty Ratified."

"The poor battered pilot" had not long to wait. The very intensity of her feeling had doubtless produced its effect, for on March 16, 1882, the Senate, with a complete and astounding unanimity, ratified and removed the injunction of secrecy from the accession of the United States to the Convention of Geneva, signed by President Arthur on March 1. A woman's single-handed fight on behalf of a great cause had ended in an amazing victory.

V

Clara Barton was now sixty-one years old, with thirty years of vigorous life still ahead of her. If she had done nothing more, her work on the battle-fields of America and Europe and her initial achievement on behalf of the Red Cross would have entitled her to a high place among American women. But she did much more, chiefly to the enlargement, partly to the diminution, of her final fame.

For its conspicuous enlargement, there was her presidency and direction of the American Red Cross for twenty-two years, from 1882 to 1904. This involved her arduous personal participation in many enterprises of active relief on fields of suffering. Dramatic and romantic incidents appear at every turn of the story, completely American in its idiom. Where but on a tributary of Mark Twain's own river could she have found a steamer with such a name as the Josh V. Throop to serve as the first American relief boat to fly the Red Cross flag? On the Ohio and Mississippi, in the river floods of 1884, she used this and another boat as floating depots of Red Cross aid. In the Texas famine of the next year she established an effective plan of self-help for the sufferers. To the summons of the Florida yellow-fever epidemic of 1888 and of the Johnstown flood of 1889 she responded with small bands of devoted helpers and large resources of supplies entrusted to her — especially at Johnstown — for distribution. After the Sea Islands hurricane of August 1893, she passed more than six months on the islands with which she had become acquainted during the siege of Charleston, directing a work of mercy among the stricken Negroes which caused them to christen their male babies "Red Cross" and the girls "Clara Barton." From Washington she had directed an expedition for the relief of the Russian famine of 1891–92. In 1895 she went herself to Constantinople in charge of succor to the survivors from an Armenian massacre, and performed a task of diplomatic delicacy with high success. In 1898 came our Spanish War, before the outbreak of which Clara Barton, at the age of seventy-seven, was in charge of a Red Cross ship at Havana, administering relief to *reconcentrados*. After war was declared, a second vessel in her charge joined Admiral Sampson's fleet off Santiago. There and in its neighborhood she supervised sanitary and hospital care of American and Cuban combatants, and was accorded the honor of sailing with her supplies into Santiago, after its surrender, in advance of the United States vessels of war. If she and her helpers joined in singing the Doxology and "America" as the State of Texas neared its dock, they need not be scorned as sentimentalists. The efficiency with which they proceeded to dispense relief to the people of Santiago marked them as eminently practical.

With all these good works, officially and universally recognized, to her credit at home, with a reputation abroad which caused the Czar of Russia in

THE JOHNSTOWN FLOOD

1902, when she was attending an International Red Cross conference in St. Petersburg, to intercept her motion to kneel and kiss his hand, by saying, "Not you, Miss Barton," it is tragic that any diminution should have touched her fame. Yet after all her provocations to self-confidence she is surely to be forgiven for not having seen what others saw — that at eighty she had held her post too long, had almost come to look upon herself as an institution, confusing what was personal and closely held in her own and few other hands with what had become national. A certain naïveté in this respect appears in words of hers about her work at the very front in Cuba: "I had not thought to make gruel again over a camp-fire. . . . I felt again that perhaps it was not in vain that history had reproduced itself." After the Galveston tornado and tidal wave of 1900, when she appeared for the last time on a scene of distress, she incurred criticism by expending Red Cross funds, as she had often done before, wholly on her own responsibility. In her book, *The Red Cross*, published in 1898, she had made what must after all be regarded as a lame defense of the financial methods she had always pursued:

On its American side it is a story of such immense success on the part of the American National Red Cross in some of its greatest and most difficult fields of labor that no financial report of them has ever been made, because the story would have been altogether incredible. The universal opinion of ordinary business people would have been that these results could not have been obtained on the means stated, and therefore something must be wrong or hidden, and to save ourselves from painful suspicion, it was decided, rightly or wrongly, that the story must remain substantially untold till its work in other fields had prepared the public mind to accept the literal truth.

This was obviously an unsound position. The Red Cross had outgrown the stage at which such methods were permissible. When Clara Barton returned from St. Petersburg in 1902 and found that the organization had done nothing for the relief of sufferers from the Mont Pelée earthquake, she blamed the inaction upon divided authority, and brought about the amendment of the by-laws increasing the powers of the president, and, just before she herself was eighty-one, accepted an election to the presidency for life. A minority of the Red Cross officials protested and became disaffected. In January 1904 the remonstrants brought about the appointment of a Congressional committee of investigation. There was of course no charge of dishonesty against Miss Barton, who had indeed always contributed largely from her own purse to the funds she dispensed, and the investigating committee was wise enough to present no report. But the American Red Cross, more than once recognized since its inception, came under a new and more broadly representative incorporation. A salaried post of honorary president for life was offered to Miss Barton and refused. The President of the United States became, in her stead, President of the Red Cross. Deeply hurt, her lifelong sensitiveness touched at a most tender point, she wrote to a California friend as one "who could, at least, tell me a road to take outside of America, and who would ask the authorities of Mexico if a woman who could not live in her own country might find a home or resting-place in theirs." She even thought of emigrating to China as another country in which the Red Cross was still to be established.

Fortunately neither of these emigrations took place. Between Oxford and Washington she passed the eight remaining years of her life, withdrawn from all Red Cross activities, but filling her energetic mind with many other interests. Two days before she died she opened her eyes and related a dream of the night before, a dream of the battle-field, on which she crept about the wounded soldiers — "trying to give them at least a drink of water to cool their parched lips, and I heard them at last speak of mother and wives and sweethearts, but never a murmur of complaint. Then I woke to hear myself groan because I have a stupid pain in my back, that's all. Here on a good bed, with every attention! I am ashamed that I murmur!" On April 12, 1912, she died, exclaiming "Let me go! Let me go!"

Clara Barton may fairly be defined as a Victorian active beyond her period. The photographs of her in the Cuban campaign as a little old lady with bonnet strings tied under her chin confirm the definition. With a simple religious faith she had none of that self-consciousness of a later time which would have hushed its avowal. Her style of writing — as when she told of "fair hands laying aside their diamonds, and business men their cares" — was often what we call Victorian. Yet she was modern enough near the end of life to respond to the beckonings of Christian Science, though never accepting it outright, and at eighty-nine to begin to learn typewriting. It is the fashion to regard Victorians with a certain contempt, to remember that, like Clara Barton, their American representatives liked beefsteak for breakfast, and to forget that their age was one in which many new ideas, subsequently translated into fact, were beginning to take form. The Red Cross idea was certainly one of these, and woman suffrage was another. Yet there is nothing distinctively Victorian in Clara Barton's expressions about women and votes — especially

with reference to war — as they appear in a letter
she wrote from Strassburg in 1870:

> Woman should certainly have some voice in the matter of
> war, either affirmative or negative, and the fact that she has
> not this should not be made the ground on which to deprive
> her of other privileges. She shan't say there will be no war,
> and she shan't take any part in it when there is one, and
> because she does n't take any part in war she must n't vote,
> and because she can't vote she has no voice in her government,
> and because she has no voice in her government she is n't a
> citizen, and because she is n't a citizen she has no rights, and
> because she has no rights she must submit to wrongs, and be-
> cause she submits to wrongs she is n't anybody.

It is a mistake to think that nobody was "modern" fifty years ago. A half century hence some of
our contemporary definitions of the term will be
hopelessly old-fashioned.

Clara Barton's formal biographers — both clergy-
men, her cousin, the Rev. W. E. Barton, and the
Rev. Percy H. Epler — would have it understood
that there were men who wished to marry her. Yet
it appears that only one led her, when she was well
advanced in life, to reciprocate this wish with any
seriousness. A white satin dress was made, and the
man at whose marriage with her it is conjectured
that the dress was to be worn, unexpectedly died,
to Miss Barton's obvious sorrow. In the face of

this mere shadow of matrimony, it is well to remember that there are celibate priests who should never have been anything else. With a family of her own it is hardly conceivable that Clara Barton should have done what she did — a unique work on the foundations of which it was possible to build an organization with 30,000,000 members in America at the end of the World War, a vastly magnified and multiplied embodiment of the Good Samaritan himself.

Between the personal and comparatively small beginnings made by Clara Barton and the gigantic operations of the American Red Cross in 1917–18 many necessary steps of systematizing, coöperation, and expansion were taken. New occasions not only teach new duties, but must present and define them. Every emergency appealing to the national instinct for effectual giving — the list is long — has enabled the successive managements of the Red Cross, now under the direction of a Central Committee, with a chairman appointed by the President of the United States, to strengthen the organization. If it depends entirely upon the popular response to a national need, that response has been never-failing. No doubt we should all sleep more comfortably in our beds if nature would forgo volcanoes and nations wars. But while such catastrophes remain possible, the American Red Cross has a function of incalculable, of constantly unpredictable, value to fulfill. For her vision of the national organization of a characteristically national impulse, for paving the way to an unspeakably useful service in the past decade, and to who knows what beyond, the name and work of Clara Barton must be reverently and gratefully remembered.

II

TOLERANCE IN RELIGION
EMBODIED IN PHILLIPS BROOKS

Four hundred and one years after Columbus discovered America the World's Fair was held in
Chicago. This was in 1893, the year in which
Phillips Brooks died at the age of fifty-seven.
One of the inscriptions which President Eliot de-
vised for the water-gate on the Court of Honor
at the Fair was in these words: "Toleration in
Religion — the Best Fruit of the Last Four Centuries." Compare the last of the four centuries
since Columbus with the first, and the change
that came about may be measured roughly by
the difference between scattered heresy-trials and
wholesale massacres. In the thirty years and
more since 1893, the spirit of toleration — always in some danger of confusion with the spirit
of indifference — might be said to have made still
more rapid advances, were it possible to ignore
the recent open conflicts between the modernists
and fundamentalists, and the hushed differences in
all the households of faith.

There is, indeed, a diminishing resort to heresy trials, for the reason that they have so often been found to settle nothing. Such a preacher as Dr. Fosdick makes no scruple to-day of exclaiming in a farewell sermon, "They call me a heretic. Well, I am a heretic if conventional orthodoxy is the standard. I should be ashamed to live in this generation and not be a heretic"; and he goes not merely unmolested but generally applauded. To-morrow it may be different. Yet the gradual and intermittent movement in matters of tolerance in religion — often dependent as it is upon the workings of individual influences in successive generations, and therefore peculiarly subject to what the Prayer Book calls the "changes and chances of this mortal life" — has been on the whole a forward movement. Differences in religious belief and practice no longer provoke so many of the "fighting words" as once proceeded from them. It has taken a long time for the world to catch up with the tolerant sentiment expressed by Benjamin Franklin when he said, "The sects are like clocks. No two agree; but they all approximate to the true time."

What, then, is the "toleration in religion" applauded in President Eliot's inscription, and what is the "tolerance in religion" with which this chapter is to concern itself? Since Phillips Brooks is the focal figure under consideration, let us turn to him for our definitions. "Tolerance," he once wrote, "is a disposition. Toleration is the behavior in which that disposition finds expression." Going a step further, he defined tolerance itself, the underlying thing, as "the willing consent that other men should hold and express opinions with which we disagree, until they are convinced by reason that those opinions were untrue."

This is a good definition: it goes on all fours, and will bear close scrutiny. The thing it defines is more a tendency than a cause, and is hardly capable of description in such concrete terms as, for example, the cause of temperance. Yet a tendency, a general movement, may have its exemplar just as recognizable as the champion of a definite cause. The whole spirit and influence of a man who represents a point of view may produce effects reaching quite as far as the results from the blows of a labeled reformer. So it was with Phillips Brooks, and it is my own belief that because he did not join or head a movement of separation, but filled with a fresh and generous spirit the old forms of the quiet faith in which he was nurtured, he set up an ideal of thought and feeling never more profitably imitable than at the present confused moment.

I

Twenty years ago a thoughtful conservative, Barrett Wendell, writing in terms of broad suggestion to a pupil, declared: "Nothing but conscious knowledge of orthodoxy could have made Emerson what he was. Those who begin with him have as yet got nowhere." There were few thinking Americans born in the first half of the nineteenth century who did not possess such a knowledge of the orthodox Protestantism of their time. This was no more true in any part of the United States than in New England, an historic centre of religious discussion and controversy. Phillips Brooks, of purely New England descent, was thirty years old at the end of our Civil War, and consequently had lived what are counted a man's formative years while the old order of thought was still regnant. In other words, he had every opportunity to acquire a conscious knowledge of orthodoxy.

It is an unhappy fact that the orthodox temper of the period in which he was born — to say nothing of the colonial times that had gone before — had many manifestations, both in disposition and in behavior, to which the word tolerance, or toleration, is quite inapplicable. Because disposition is expressed in behavior, and because it is impossible to appreciate the spirit of tolerance of which Phillips Brooks was an inspiring representative without some knowledge of the contrasting spirit of intolerance, — especially in the years immediately preceding his active life, — it will be well to set in array a few "behavioristic" instances. They are merely symptoms of the withholding of that willing consent to differences of opinion on which tolerance is based, tokens of that insistence on conformity, sometimes by minorities, out of which, in all churches and at all times, conflicts and persecutions have risen. It is of secondary consequence that most of the instances are related to the transition from the rigors of Calvinistic theology to the less austere modes of religious thought that accompanied the broadening of scientific and other horizons in the nineteenth century. The merits of the several cases are less to the present purpose than the temper and behavior which they provoked.

But before reverting to the American past, let us remind ourselves that in the boyhood of Edmund

Gosse, born nearly fifteen years after Phillips Brooks, it was possible in England for a sensitive youth, undergoing the painful process of separation from the extreme Calvinistic views of his father, to hear a speaker at an evangelical conference announce with all solemnity: "At this very moment there is proceeding, unreproved, a blasphemous celebration of the birth of Shakespeare, a lost soul now suffering for his sins in hell." This was hardly a typical utterance of the eighteen-sixties, but the man who made it stood by no means entirely alone.

The confident assigning of the unregenerate — or the dissentient — to eternal punishment was the stock in trade of many zealots, on both sides of the Atlantic. At Hanover, New Hampshire, in 1835, a traveling evangelist interrupted a service for Dartmouth College students by greeting a respectable local attorney, late in entering the meeting-house, after the fashion of certain evangelists in all times: "Here comes another miserable sinner going straight to hell." The annals of Dartmouth College itself preserve a more dignified but no less significant expression of religious prejudice in the same year of 1835. In that year a professorship of chemistry and mineralogy was abolished, and in the year following restored under the new designation of chemistry, mineralogy, and geology. Why? Because the man who held the first professorship was an Episcopalian, even in deacon's orders, and, though an excellent teacher, was so distasteful to the college authorities on the score of his church affiliations that the shortest and surest road to getting rid of him — by abolishing the post he occupied — was adopted.

It is a short step from New Hampshire into Maine, and from 1835 to 1840, in which year the town of Augusta, Maine, was the theatre of an extraordinary tragi-comedy of religious persecution. The story of it is told in a little book, now of great rarity, printed in Augusta in 1841, under the title, *Scenes in a Vestry: Being an account of the late controversy in the South Parish Congregational Church in Augusta, Reported by D. C. Weston, Esq.* The circumstances it records are those that followed the adoption of the report of a parish committee in 1840, supporting warmly some recent resolutions of the parish against dancing, and the prompt defiance of this position by a spirited and highly respected older member of the parish, Mrs. Nathan Weston. Not only did she permit the members of the "Winter Circle," a benevolent sewing society of "misses between the ages of ten and fifteen," to dance in her house with boys who joined them after their sewing was done, her son and daughter providing the music of violin and piano for the occasion, but when a deacon urged her to be controlled in her opinions and practice by the actions of the church in the matter of dancing, she declared she "would rather be ground to powder first." She maintained, moreover, that, as a lifelong student of the Holy Book, she had "been unable to find anything there which forbids, either in direct terms or by fair implication, children or others to move their limbs responsive to music." When she and her husband, Judge Weston, announced their withdrawal from the South Parish Church to take up more congenial religious associations, "the impropriety of an attempt to withdraw from a Christian church without its consent" was solemnly urged, and the persecution of the offenders, including the piano-playing daughter, who had fallen seriously ill over the whole affair, was continued. This daughter, by the way, became the mother of Chief Justice Fuller, of the United States Supreme Court. The pettiness and cruelty of the entire episode seem to-day incredible.

In Andover, Massachusetts, where the maternal forbears of Phillips Brooks established the Academy and Seminary from which the soundest orthodoxy has proceeded, there are many traditions of the old-time intensity of theological differences. (Apropos of the fact that the early Phillipses were not invariably harmonious amongst themselves, a jocular saying of Phillips Brooks himself is recalled by a friend, to the effect that he liked to think of these ancestors as of the foundations under his house — glad that they are there, and glad also that they are out of sight.) It is told of the Andover professors that, besides fighting the battles of orthodoxy in the larger world, they expressed their own conflicts of opinion in the Seminary pulpit. Thus it could happen that when a teacher of the more progressive sort expounded his views before the divinity students in the sermon of one Sunday, the preacher on the next Sunday was capable of holding him up to scorn. "The atheist says this"; "The infidel says that"; "The man who does not pray maintains" — and so forth, quoting from the preacher of the week before. To the credit of the human nature persisting in that eminent divine, occupying a front seat in the chapel while thus subjected to ridicule, the story has it that he would turn his back to the preacher, his face to the congregation of students, and stick out his tongue in reciprocal contempt. Some of the ways of piety were strange indeed.

STATUE OF PHILLIPS BROOKS BY BELA PRATT
AT NORTH ANDOVER. MASSACHUSETTS

In *Old Andover Days*, written by a daughter of
the humorous theologian, the extreme strictness
of Sabbath observance on "the Hill" is set forth
with depressing, though illuminative, detail. Yet
no item of it was more significant than the true
story of a Boston journalist who, on his appointment more than fifty years ago as managing editor of the respectable daily paper with which
he was connected, received a solemn warning
from the deacons of the suburban orthodox church
he had faithfully attended that if he gave any
of the hours of Sunday afternoon and evening to
the preparation of the Monday morning's paper
his membership in the church must cease. Did
they read the Monday paper? he asked his in-
quisitors. Oh yes, they replied, but not on Sunday; that was different. The editor accordingly
took refuge in another denomination, with which
a venerable great-uncle of my own was identified
as a bishop. In his old age, which came before
the reading of Sunday newspapers grew general,
one of the faithful protested against his taking
up this profane practice, for which he could offer
no stronger defense than the quavering words,
"But I must follow the Lord's dealings with the
children of men!"

These are trivialities, and valuable only — but

really valuable — for the light they throw on the temper of a past time. When important matters were afoot, there was abundant seriousness. Take such a case as that of Frederic Dan Huntington, in his early manhood a most popular Unitarian preacher and Harvard professor, in his later life the Protestant Episcopal Bishop of Central New York. When he left the Unitarian denomination in 1860, he received from one of his brothers, a judge in Western Massachusetts, a letter quite characteristic of its period. "The 'Church,' " the brother wrote, "has always seemed to me a snug harbor, a quiet retreat, a safe religious asylum for well-disposed people who shudder at all the 'isms' of the day, and conscientiously desire to say their prayers in a social, respectable way, and to bring up their children in the nurture and admonition of the Lord, and of their godfathers and godmothers, and to compound for a general weekday indulgence in the fashions, pleasures, and vanities of the world by a steady observance of the set days, the new moons, the feasts, and the fasts, and the fish-days."[1] It was bad enough for a Unitarian

---

[1] It is no wonder that such opinions of the Episcopal Church existed when it is remembered that an Anglican visitor to New York in 1828 wrote of a service at Grace Church: "The appearance of the congregation was highly respectable; indeed it appeared to contain none of the lower classes of society." See *America and the American Church*, by the Rev. Henry Caswall, p. 11.

to substitute any such new asylum of faith for his old; but had he become an orthodox Congregationalist, a still stronger prejudice on his Unitarian brother's part would have faced him. Of this denomination, the brother wrote in the same letter: "As a body, with their hypocrisy, bigotry, exclusive creed, pharisaic spirit, their clean outside cups and platters and sepulchres, and intolerant and persecuting temper, I think they are about as poor a commentary upon the meek, loving, charitable, and gentle spirit of Christianity as could well be got up."

Or take the later case of the Rev. Dr. George A. Gordon, at the time of his installation, in 1884, as minister of the Old South Church in Boston. The cross-examination to which he was subjected by a Council of sixty-six Congregational ministers and deacons was a trial of orthodoxy almost worthy of the days of Anne Hutchinson. Only she was banished to the wilds of Rhode Island, and Dr. Gordon, approved by a vote of forty-eight to eighteen, was installed in the ministry he has adorned for more than forty years.

They cared very much — all these defenders of the faith once delivered to the saints. After their own fashion they did their best to fulfill "the chief end of man" by glorifying God. In the exercise of their other function, "to enjoy Him forever," they started sometimes on surprising paths.

II

Phillips Brooks was primarily and completely a preacher. Preaching, as he regarded it, was "the bringing of truth through personality." "The sermon," he said, "is truth and man together. It is the truth brought through the man." Before considering the truth he brought to his generation, let us look at the man and his personality.

In the matter of outward circumstance, his life was as uneventful as that of any conspicuous clergyman can be. He was born in Boston, December 13, 1835. At the Boston Latin School he made his preparation for Harvard College, from which he graduated in the class of 1855. After a brief, disastrous attempt at teaching in the Boston Latin School, he entered the Theological Seminary at Alexandria, Virginia, and for three years pursued his studies for the ministry of the Protestant Episcopal Church. Then for two years, from 1859 to 1861, he was rector of the Church of the Advent in Philadelphia, a small parish in the northern part of the city. From 1861 to 1869 he held the rectorship of Holy Trinity Church, Rittenhouse Square, Philadelphia. In 1869, after much hesitation, he resigned this position to become rector of Trinity Church, Boston, in the ministry of which he continued until he became Bishop of Massachusetts in 1891. Less than two years later, on January 23, 1893, he died. In the course of his life he employed every vacation opportunity for extensive travel — in Europe and the Holy Land, to India and Japan. At various times he might have turned to other work than preaching — as a divinity-school teacher in Philadelphia or Cambridge, as president of a Church college in Ohio, as a Harvard professor, as assistant Bishop of Pennsylvania. When the end of his life was at hand, he accepted the bishopric of Massachusetts only under the strongest impulsion of duty.

Such are the bare facts of his career. To the secretary of his college class, demanding information for an anniversary report, he wrote, late in his life: "I have had no wife, no children, no particular honors, no serious misfortunes, and no adventures worth speaking of. It is shameful at such times as these not to have a history; but I have not got one, and must come without." What his record did possess was a singular unity. To be a unit in personality and life — that is, to show qualities of the same sort throughout —

is a frequent, though of course not invariable, token of greatness. Phillips Brooks was strikingly a unit, without the contradictions in his nature and its expression which in many other men call for reconciliation. This oneness appears first of all in his personality.

What he was and what he did were so interwoven that the two things can hardly be separated. His inheritances and their influence upon him were, however, beyond his control, and their contribution to his personality was marked. His father, a man of high probity and intelligence, through his whole active life a hardware merchant in Boston, came of the Massachusetts family of Brooks, chiefly identified in the generations before him with the successful handling of practical affairs. "They were honored, trusted, and loved," says Dr. Allen, the biographer of Phillips Brooks, "in each passing generation." Back of them ancestrally, through an eighteenth-century marriage, stood the Reverend John Cotton, a dominating clerical figure of Boston in its earliest days, the "very great-grandfather" of whom Phillips Brooks once declared: "I thank him as a Church of England man, as a man loving the Episcopal Church with all my heart, I thank him for being a Puritan."

Touching Puritanism itself there are other words of Phillips Brooks illustrating the humorous apprehension of many things which was a positive element in his make-up. "It stands," he said, "like a rusty gun in a corner of the room; but let no man ever fool with Puritanism, thinking the thing is not loaded, for by and by it will go off. . . . I suppose the real proof that we are Puritans is that we are proud of being Puritans; which nobody but a Puritan would be."

The Brookses turned from Orthodoxy to Unitarianism in time for Phillips Brooks's father to grow up in it. Not so the Phillips family, the founders and benefactors of the Phillips Academies at Andover and Exeter, from whom the mother of Phillips Brooks derived her name and descent. The Puritanism of a long line of preachers antedating these foundations ran strong in her veins. Mrs. William Gray Brooks (Mary Ann Phillips), the mother of six sons, four of whom entered the ministry of the Episcopal Church, was concerned quite as deeply throughout their boyhood for their spiritual as for their physical welfare. This feeling doubtless played its part in the early separation of Phillips Brooks's parents from the Unitarian Church in which they began their married life, and the transfer of their allegiance to the Episcopal parish of St. Paul's in Boston. Here they and their growing family of boys found abundant satisfaction in the religious influences which formed a vital part of the family life.

The ineradicable Puritanism of the mother revealed itself strangely from time to time. There is a story of her hearing her two sons, Phillips and Frederick, after they had become rectors of important churches respectively in Philadelphia and Cleveland, laughing unrestrainedly together on a Sunday visit to their parents, and coming to the doorway of the room in which they sat to warn them with, "Boys, remember it is Sunday." There was a time, moreover, while Phillips Brooks was still in Philadelphia, when his mother feared the effect of Horace Bushnell's writings upon his orthodoxy. "Philly," she wrote to him, "they are nothing better than Unitarianism that I suffered under all my young life. . . . I hope you do not own the book called 'Christ and His Salvation.' But if you do I want you to burn it with Frederick present to witness and exult over it. I have no patience with the book or with the man."

When her most eminent son was first taking his place as a distinguished preacher, she wrote him another letter containing these pathetic sentences:

"Sometimes I really feel that nothing but the mother's love remains in me. That will never cease, for the dead or the living. And Philly, often now, truly I don't feel quite *equal* to writing to you. You have got *before* me now, and this is the course of all nature. The old stalk is good for nothing after it has yielded its fruit. Just so it is with you and me." Between the mother and son no such divergence as she feared ever came to pass. When she died in 1880 Phillips Brooks wrote to his friend, Dr. Weir Mitchell, "My mother has been the centre of all the happiness of my life. Thank God she is not less my pride and treasure now." Writing at the same time to his brother Arthur, "The Brooks boys have got to stand together as long as they are left," he gave further token of that depth of family affection, and indeed of all personal loyalties, which must be counted among his strongest individual traits. These loyalties were many, and among them his friendships — springing from the relations of school, college, seminary, and the ministry — held always an important place. In the circle of his sympathies the unfortunate and the burdened, and especially the children, with all the satisfaction or the pathos of ultimate adjustments to living still in store for them, were warmly enclosed. No more touching and illuminating picture of his relations with a child can be found than in the autobiography of Helen Keller, the eyes of whose soul he did so much to open.

"Every true preacher," he once said, "must be a poet"; and quite apart from his own adventures in verse, in which feeling and felicity are both to be found, the vein of poetry that ran through all his prose accounted for a marked and appealing element of beauty in his sermons. The creative imagination of the poet is suggested, moreover, in such a bit of testimony as that of a director of charities in Trinity Church, Boston. It was her custom to give him from time to time a list of poor women in distress that he might visit and pray with them. Especially those who had lost young children would come to her afterwards and say, "How can he know so well just how I feel?"

With the poetic sense went a sense of proportion — by no means always an attribute of poets. In the case of Phillips Brooks this was doubtless related to a sound and pervading sense of humor, and perhaps also in some degree to an early experience of utter failure.

The best sense of humor is that which enables

its possessor to join in a laugh at his own expense. If Phillips Brooks, six feet four inches in height, had not possessed this endowment, it is doubtful whether he would have been willing, as a member of the Hasty Pudding Club at Harvard, to take part in Fielding's "Tragedy of Tragedies, or the Life and Death of Tom Thumb the Great," in which he enacted the rôle of "Glumdalca of the Giants, a captive Queen, beloved by the King, but in love with Tom Thumb." The incongruities of word and action resulting from this union of Fielding and the future bishop have an *ex post facto* humor not to be ignored. Another good sign of his unwillingness as an undergraduate to take himself too seriously is found in the pleasure he is reported to have taken in telling an anecdote of his instruction in English composition by Professor Child. He had written a college exercise of which the opening portion had all the elaboration of "fine writing" and greatly pleased him. It was good for his acquisition of the writer's art, though bad for his self-esteem at the moment, to have Professor Child return the paper with the penciled words, at the end of the introduction, "Begin here." (William Everett, his college junior by four years, may have profited by the same methods, for when he became an instructor in

English himself, he is said to have poured even colder water upon a student who submitted a written exercise in verse instead of the expected prose. Everett, as the story runs, looked at it a moment, and then asked, "But, why begin every line with a capital letter?")

Whatever chastening of early exuberance Brooks may have received in college, he must have got a great deal more out of his attempts, in the year after his graduation, to become a teacher in the Boston Latin School. This had to be abandoned when the school year was half done. The giantess of the Pudding play had proved a dwarf in the practice of discipline. The boys in his charge would pack the thermometer with ice, bringing the recorded temperature of the schoolroom so low that they would demand and receive permission to stuff the stove with wood, until the heat became intolerable. They threw shot in the teacher's face, scattered explosive match-heads over the floor, equipped themselves with mock eye-glasses made of scraps of tin, and once subjected their victim to the ignominy of being locked into the schoolroom, from which he escaped only by lowering a boy out of the window to clear the keyhole of the obstructions that plugged it. The situation was impossible; and the humiliation of resigning his post was not diminished by the dictum of Francis Gardner, master of the Latin School, that a man who failed in teaching could never succeed in anything else. In later years Brooks, who had himself been one of Gardner's pupils, paid him a generous tribute as a teacher. How completely he filled that rôle may be gathered from the story that when he was taken to hear Phillips Brooks, at the height of his powers, preach in Boston, his only remark upon the sermon called attention to the ungrammatical construction of a sentence.

The ineffectual teacher may be a prodigious learner, and from his failure in one effort Brooks certainly learned the direction in which to look for success in another. His elders to whom he turned for guidance advised the ministry, towards which the nature of his wide reading in college, in addition to his domestic influences, seemed clearly to point the way. One of his advisers was the Reverend Dr. A. H. Vinton, to whom Brooks, betraying his own innate reticence, used to protest in later years, "It was mean of you to get a fellow in a corner and throw his soul at him." This bore its part, however, in sending him to the Theological Seminary at Alexandria, a school of "evangelical" churchmanship, where the young

New Englander had his first experience of fervent students who led him to observe that "the boiler had no connection with the engine." Many adaptations, educative in their total effect, ensued. His abilities as a speaker, at the Seminary and in a near-by chapel to which he ministered, were fully realized, even though one of his fellow students declared, apropos of his first sermon, on the text, "The simplicity that is in Christ," that "there was very little simplicity in the sermon and no Christ." It was entirely like Brooks to see the point and the humor of the criticism. When he left the Seminary it was with all the markings of a man of promise.

For more than thirty years the fulfillment of this promise went steadily forward. The personality, the notable individuality, with which the process began grew only more distinctive with the passage of time; yet it was all one thing, a unit, growing to the last. The frame and the spirit of the man were perfectly matched. The bodily proportions of heroic size, the beauty, nobility, and distinction of countenance, were in complete harmony with the generosity of mind and soul to which tongue and pen gave expression. The flood of thought and feeling on the central matter of religion — which he regarded simply as "the life of man in gratitude and obedience and gradually developing likeness to God" — needed the outlet of a torrent; and in his speech, the despair of stenographers, since it came at the rate of two hundred or more words a minute instead of the average speaker's one hundred and twenty, that outlet was amazingly found. Fortunate the message which had such a bearer.

Since Phillips Brooks was committed neither by vows nor by natural affiliations to any theory of a celibate clergy, many have found it matter of wonder and regret that marriage and a family life of his own did not enter into his personal experience. This lack he would doubtless have deplored himself, had he been given to self-revelings. "The trouble with you married men," he was wont, according to his biographer, to say, "is that you think no one has been in love but yourselves," and to claim for himself a knowledge of this common lot. Between the lines of Dr. Allen's abridged biography it may be clearly read that before he left Philadelphia the possibility and the hope of matrimony were in his mind. In describing the circumstances that led to his reconsideration of the call from Philadelphia to Boston, Dr. Allen writes: "A change had taken place in the situation. The personal issue which had made

Phillips Brooks hesitant and vacillating had been determined." After all these years it is no invasion of personal privacy — indeed it enhances the human quality of the man — to recognize his failure to persuade the person to whom he gave his affections to share his life, and to find in the fact that he did not bestow them elsewhere a token of that unity and wholeness which marked all his thought and action.

When he came to Boston his local fame rested largely upon the prayer he had made in July 1865, at the Harvard Commemoration of the Civil War — an utterance that produced the deepest impression even of the day for which Lowell prepared his Commemoration Ode. The war and a profound appreciation of the greatness of Lincoln had stirred young Brooks to the depths of his being, and affected for life his sense of citizenship in a country claiming his pride and devotion. His method of serving it was through the enrichment of individual lives. In his volumes of *Essays and Addresses, Religious, Literary, and Social*, it may be seen how freely he gave himself to the larger interests of his community.

It is noticeable, however, and suggestive of a personal characteristic, that he did not identify himself with this or that specific reform, but devoted his thought and influence to the fundamental things out of which human betterment in many phases may be expected to grow. A significant incident is preserved in the story of a clergyman, perplexed over some problems of his work, who went to Brooks for advice and came away saying to himself, "We did n't discuss any of the things I came to ask about, but I think I know now how to tackle them." Thus in private and in public relations the young clergyman whose prayer at Harvard caused many an astonished hearer to ask, "Who is this?" became by steady degrees one of the landmark figures of his time and place.

In a sense he never grew old — not even for the fifty-seven years he had reached when death overtook him. In this respect his essential sympathy with children and young people — "the best people in the world," he called them — may have been either cause or effect. To the students of Harvard College, which he served enthusiastically both as an overseer and as a preacher — and refrained from serving as a professor only after the gravest thought — his devotion was deep and constant. The feeling of these students for him, memorably revealed on the day of his burial by their silent array as the funeral procession passed through the College Yard on its way from Boston to Mount Auburn, was the ultimate tribute to his freedom from all taint of sham or professionalism.

Eagerly going about his work throughout life, he never took his dignities and triumphs with that seriousness which encumbers smaller men. While the confirmation of his election to the episcopate awaited the approval of a majority of the bishops in the Episcopal Church, and the air was filled with talk of opposition on grounds of heterodoxy, his refusal to justify himself otherwise than by reference to his published writings betokened the dignity on which he really stood. The persistent boyishness of the man came out, after his consecration, when, attending for the first and last time a meeting of the House of Bishops, he whispered to his old Seminary friend, Bishop Potter of New York, "Henry, is it always as dull as this?" and wrote in a letter to one of his nieces, "The bishops are not very wise, but they think they are, and they very much enjoy being bishops." Indeed he enjoyed being a bishop himself, not for any factitious advantages, but because he truly found in this most exalted service of the Church he loved a promise for the greatest opportunity of usefulness that could have come to him. If his fellow bishops amused him, he did not exempt himself, as one of them, from a humorous scrutiny. When his friend McVickar, afterwards Bishop of Rhode Island, said to him one day while they were traveling together in Switzerland, "It is strange, Brooks, to think of you as a bishop," he made reply, "It is so strange, Willie, that sometimes when I am putting on my clothes I have to stop and laugh."

The place that Phillips Brooks came to occupy in the affectionate and admiring confidence of his contemporaries at home and abroad, of all creeds and conditions, indeed wherever he carried his message, became a place so hung with the garlands of praise, especially after his death, that those who belong to a later generation can hardly believe all the praise to have been merited. Was it the truth he proclaimed that won him this place, or the personality through which the truth was transmitted? That towering personality, unique in its constant suggestion that some of the elements of its greatness were attainable by all, surely exerted a spell of a potency all its own.

III

If a man's personality eludes satisfactory description, the truth proclaimed in a lifetime of preaching is no more a simple thing to summarize. Phillips Brooks's reply to the question about the sermon he was going to preach one day in England, "Oh, I have only one sermon," seems — but merely seems — to simplify the matter. His one sermon, to be sure, may be said to have had for its object the demonstration of religion, under his definition of it as "nothing in the world but the highest conception of life." This sermon in its hundreds of forms presented the reality, naturalness, and simplicity of the relation between men and God, a loving Father, a Son and Brother, both human and divine, a Spirit capable of guiding and comforting the lives of human beings — all a mystery, definable in terms of poetry more nearly than in those of science.

Phillips Brooks was not deeply learned in the formal theologies and philosophies. His thinking on theological matters was influenced in largest measure by the writings of Coleridge, Horace Bushnell, and Frederick Denison Maurice. His extensive reading in general literature — not least in poetry — and the breadth, both native and cultivated, of his own human sympathies, affected, more than any intensive study of philosophy, the apprehension of life expressed in his preaching. His intellectual and spiritual temper was that of the poet, the mystic, the symbolist, as opposed to the literalist and realist, not yet in his day known as the fundamentalist.

The translation of volumes of his sermons and essays into German, French, and Dutch bears evidence to an element of universal appeal in his utterances. His sermons in English have had many, though naturally a diminishing number of readers since his death. For the very reason that in sermons the truth that is preached and the personality of the preacher are so interdependent, it is hardly to be expected that one may derive today from his sermons so clear and characteristic an impression of his personality as from his other writings. Is it not true that the subtraction of personality does more to injure a sermon than almost any other form of original expression? The better a sermon is, the more, perhaps, it requires the actual medium of its creator's utterance. Be that as it may, the reader of this later time who wishes to acquaint himself with the spirit of Phillips Brooks and the springs of his power cannot do better than to read his collected *Essays and Addresses* (1894), his *Lectures on Preaching* (1877), his lectures on *The Influence of Jesus* (1879), and particularly his two lectures to divinity students published in a little volume under the title of

Tolerance (1887). As the subject of that book — in many respects a spiritual autobiography — is the subject of this paper, it will illustrate finally both the general and the personal topic of present concern to see what the book contains.

There is one passage in it so suggestive of the religious and human sympathies which permeated the thought and effort of Phillips Brooks that it should not be given wholly in summary. It presents his conception of "every man who truly values his place in the Christian Church" as called upon to think of himself "standing in the midst of four concentric circles," he the centre of them all, they representing the different horizons of his life. What are these circles?

Outermost of all, there is the broad circle of humanity. All men, simply as men, are something to this man. It is the consciousness, "*Homo sum,*" the consciousness which the Latin poet crowded into his immortal line, which fills this circle with vitality. Next within this is the circle of religion, smaller than the other, because all men are not religious, but large enough to include all those of every name, of every creed, who count this life the subject and the care of a Divine life which is their king. Next within this circle lies the circle of Christianity, including all those, who, under any conception of Him and of their duty to Him, honestly own for their master Jesus Christ. And then, inmost of all, there is the circle of the man's own peculiar Church, the group of those whose thought and worship is in general identical with his who stands in the centre and feels all these four circles surrounding him.

This philosophy of human relationships — obviously applicable in other fields than that of religion — is capable also of the broadest personal application. "I cannot live truly with the men of my own Church," said Phillips Brooks, "unless I also have a consciousness of common life with all Christian believers, with all religious men, with all mankind."

The man who stands at the centre of the four spreading circles is he who can best illustrate in his life the definition of tolerance quoted near the beginning of this paper: "the willing consent that other men should hold and express opinions with which we disagree, until they are convinced by reason that those opinions were untrue." The little volume, *Tolerance*, from which these and the preceding words are taken, is, in the field of religion, a very charter of the subject. Let a few scattered quotations from its pages speak for its spirit:

[Of tolerance] It is composed of two elements, both of which are necessary to its true existence, and on the harmonious and proportionate blending of which the quality of tolerance which is the result, depends. These elements are, first, positive conviction; and, second, sympathy with men whose convictions differ from our own.

True tolerance consists in the love of truth and the love of man, each brought to its perfection and living in perfect harmony with one another; but . . . these two great affections are perfect and in perfect harmony only when they are orbed and enfolded in the yet greater affection of the love of God. . . . The boy of whom the stranger asked the way to Farmington is the very image of the love of man that is not mingled and harmonized with love for truth. "It is eight miles," the boy replied. "Are you sure that it is so far as that?" the weary traveler asked. The boy, with his big heart overrunning with the milk of human kindness, looked at him and replied, "Well, seeing that you are pretty tired, I will call it seven miles." How much of would-be tolerance has sounded in our ears like that!

The tolerance which is patient toward what it counts honest error is utterly impatient toward dishonesty, toward hypocrisy, toward self-conceit, toward cant, whether it be on the side of what the honest man thinks to be error, or of that which he thinks to be true.

The real unity of Christendom is not to be found at last in identity of organization, nor in identity of dogma. Both of these have been dreamed of, and have failed. But in the unity of spiritual consecration to a common Lord — so earnestly sought by every soul that, though their apprehension of Him whom they are seeking shall be as various as are the lights into which a hundred jewels break the selfsame sunlight — the search shall be so deep a fact, so much the deepest fact in every soul, that all the souls shall be one with each other in virtue of that simple fact, in virtue of that common reaching after Christ, that common earnestness of loyalty to what they know of him. There is the only unity that is thoroughly worthy either of God or man.

After you have conquered or outgrown all your unwillingness that men should think in enterprising and dangerous ways, you turn and look in upon yourself, only to find your soul full of uncharitable thoughts towards men who still are keeping the reluctance you used to feel. Until you get rid of those thoughts you are not fully tolerant.

So long as any Church is aware that there are Christians to whom she, as she is now constituted, cannot open her doors, she must be more than content — she must be thankful and rejoice — that there are forms of worship and groups of believers in which those Christians for whom she has no place may find fellowship with one another and feed their souls with truth.

A multitude of men to-day have abandoned the idea of persecuting their brethren for their opinions, only because they either, on the one hand, have seen the hopelessness and uselessness of it, or else, upon the other hand, have been willing to leave the punishment of the errorist to God. That sort of tolerance is superficial and unstable. The only ground for us to take is the broad ground that error is not punishable at all. Error is not guilt. The guilt of error is the fallacy and fiction which has haunted good men's minds.

How quickly one discovers as one goes about in the strange,

windy world of protestants, reformers, radicals, philanthro-
pists, and denouncers of the world's innumerable wrongs,
which are the few among the multitude who have kept their
power of moral indignation pure by using it only at the right
times and on the right material. How they shine like clear
stars in the midst of the lurid light of all the rest!

Tolerance does not mean the forgetting of differences, but
the clear recognition of them and the hearty acceptance and
use of them.

Be more afraid of the littleness than of the largeness of life.

IV

All these words were written nearly forty years
ago, and, in so far as their drift is concerned,
Phillips Brooks might have written them ten or
twenty years earlier. They do not sound at all
old-fashioned to-day, but express principles of religion and life which are precisely as applicable
now that the twentieth century is well begun as
they were long before the nineteenth ended. And
in this fact the secret of his hold upon his own
generation may well be found. One may now see
that his contemporaries must have felt through
him a contemporaneity with the best in times past
and to come. It was no mere wish to say a pleas-
ant thing that led the Roman Catholic Arch-
bishop Ryan of Philadelphia to declare after

Brooks's death: "I knew Phillips Brooks only
by character and his writings. He was one of
those men whom you feel you ought to have
known, and regret that you did not. His truly
broad catholic heart, and splendid, luminous intellect have left their impression for good on the
whole country." It was not an ecclesiastic, but
a physician, novelist, and poet, Dr. Weir Mitchell,
also a dear friend of Phillips Brooks, who wrote
of him, "I have known a number of men we call
great, — poets, statesmen, soldiers, — but Phillips
was the only one I ever knew who seemed to me
entirely great." The generation that knew him
not must take the word of that which knew him.
Those who cannot hear his voice when they read
his sermons may not care to read them. Indeed
the reading of any sermons is an obsolescent pas-
time. But the voice of tolerance is one to which
the world is bound to listen more and more, and
in that voice Phillips Brooks, through a far-ex-
tending influence, will long be heard.

THE LONG DRIVE FOR TEMPERANCE

WITH THE HELP OF FRANCES E. WILLARD

AND surely it is time (yea more than tyme) that we should foresee, and learne to avoyde, those Mermaydes of myschiefe, which pype so pleasantly in every Potte, that men be thereby allured to sayle into the Ilandes of all evyle.

WITH all the authority of a tosspot famous in his day George Gascoigne wrote these words — in *A delicate Diet, for daintiemouthde Droonkardes* — as long ago as 1576. Let us not go back so far, however, to recover a still more significant reminder that the perils attending the intemperate use of intoxicating drink have been realized for a long time even here in America, and, furthermore, that national prohibition was not suddenly "put over" on the American public. This reminder is found in words ascribed to Abraham Lincoln on the very day of his assassination: "After reconstruction the next great work before us is the prohibition of the liquor traffic in all the States and Territories." Did he really say this? According to the Honorable Charles E. Littlefield of Maine, speaking at the dedication of the statue to Frances E. Willard in the national Capitol on February 17, 1905, he did. But the historical evidence in support of any such definite statement is unsatisfying. What cannot be questioned is that as early as 1842, in a temperance speech at Springfield, Illinois, on Washington's Birthday, Lincoln had rejoiced in the prospect of a day "when there shall be neither a slave nor a drunkard on the earth," and on the same occasion made this characteristic utterance: "Let us make it as unfashionable to withhold our names from the temperance cause as for husbands to wear their wives' bonnets to church, and instances will be just as rare in the one case as in the other." The claims of the advocates of temperance that Lincoln was with them, in principle and practice, rest indeed upon a firm foundation.

The drive for this cause, engaging many ardent workers before and during Lincoln's association with it, experienced more than one burst of momentum in his lifetime. In the sixty years since his death, prohibition has become — with consequences which he could hardly have foreseen — the law of the land. In bringing this to pass the women of the country, notably personified in Frances E. Willard, have borne an important part. The story now to be told has to do with the cause both before and after her identification with it, and also with the strange personal force of that identification.

I

The problem of drink and its effect upon society appears to have caused no particular anxiety until the use of distilled, rather than fermented, liquors became general. In England gin — or Geneva waters, so named not from the city of Calvin, the Red Cross, and the League of Nations, but from a word signifying juniper — was the greatest troublemaker. Home-brewed gin became so cheap in the eighteenth century that spirit-bars in London are said to have displayed signs inviting the passer-by to be "drunk for one penny," or "dead drunk for 2*d*," with the generous provision for "sleeping it off" on "straw for nothing." In these conditions it can hardly be questioned that liquor legislation became a need of the times. In the New World penalties had already been made to fit the crime. The Massachusetts Colony records as early as 1634 tell of one Robert Coles sentenced for drunkenness "to be disfranchised," — a modern paraphrase of the verdict is quoted, — "and to wear about his neck, and to hang about his outer garment a *D* made of red cloth, set upon white, to continue for a year and not to leave it off at any time when he

Wo to Drunkards.

TWO

SERMONS

Teſtifying againſt the Sin of

Drunkenneſs:

WHEREIN

The Wofulneſs of that Evil, and the
Miſery of all that are Addicted to it, is
Diſcovered from the WORD of GOD.

By Increaſe Mather, D.D.

The Second Edition.

Habakkuk II. 15.

Wo unto him that giveth his Neighbour Drink:
That putteſt thy Bottle to him, and makeſt
him Drunken alſo.

BOSTON:

Printed and Sold by Timothy Green, at the
Lower End of Middle-Street, 1712.

The Nature and Effects of Drunken-
neſs conſidered ; with an Addreſs to
Tavern-Keepers, to Parents, and
young People, relating to the Subject,

IN

Two DISCOURSES.

Delivered at NATICK, the laſt Lord's Day in
October, 1773.

By STEPHEN BADGER, A. M.

Paſtor of the CHRISTIAN SOCIETY there.

Publiſh'd by Deſire of the Hearers and others.

BOSTON:

Printed for EDES and GILL, in QUEEN-STREET,
1774.

VOICES AGAINST INTEMPERANCE FROM THE EIGHTEENTH CENTURY
NEW ENGLAND PULPIT

should come among company." In Virginia, by no means a Puritan colony, a certain Robert Warder was sentenced, for getting drunk, to stand at the door of Nassawattocks Church, Northampton County, "with a great pot tied about his neck."

There was indeed plenty of occasion to deal drastically with the drinking usage of Americans through the seventeenth and eighteenth centuries, though it was not until the nineteenth that any organized effort towards reform was undertaken. The habits that were carried over into that century were rooted deep in the social life of the people. It is significant that so serious an occasion as a college commencement became so riotous and disorderly a holiday, not only for the academic but for the general public, that before the middle of the eighteenth century the Corporation of Harvard College used to try to keep the exact date of Commencement Day a secret. Even a hundred years later a good New England minister who attended some sixty Harvard Commencements and recorded the annual happenings in his diary, made note, in 1835, that "by my suggestion also, as thanks are commonly returned after dinner when there is great hilarity, and it is difficult to restore order, the usual Psalm LXXVIII was substituted . . . St. Martin's, which I set the

23d time, went well." The humor of engaging the
noisy graduates in singing a psalm instead of expect-
ing them to cease from disorder during "grace after
meat" appears to have escaped the diarist.

If so respectable an institution as the oldest college in America was thus disturbed by alcohol —
and the disturbances are barely suggested here —
the churches themselves were not exempt. When
the frame of a meeting-house was raised in a New
England town in 1793, the selectmen merely con-
formed with the custom of the time in providing
two barrels of rum, which was considered "licker
sufficient for the spectators." The social ceremonies
attending even such an event as the ordination of a
minister at Plymouth gave the Reverend Lyman
Beecher, the father of Henry Ward Beecher and Mrs.
Stowe, occasion to observe that "the sideboard with
the spillings of water, and sugar, and liquor, looked
and smelled like the bar of a very active grog-shop."
Farther to the South and somewhat earlier, the
usages of society are suggested in the record of an
Italian traveler, Mazzei:

In 1774, finding myself one day at Norfolk at a dinner of
thirty-two people, and having asked for a glass of water, I
perceived some confusion among the servants, and the water
did not arrive. The host, next whom I sat, whispered in my

ear, asking with a smile if I could not drink something else, because the unexpected request for a glass of water had upset the entire household and they did not know what they were about.

These concrete instances are cited merely to indicate the extent to which American life, in all the gradations of the social scale, was flavored with alcohol. In many families which have existed as such for a century or more the lavish inheritance of decanters is a tangible reminder of the days when these vessels stood regularly refilled upon the sideboard instead of perpetually empty on a pantry shelf. All that they imply with regard to old-time social relations had an inevitable counterpart in moral and economic conditions.

With the coming of the nineteenth century, — why has it not been labeled "the Century of Reform"? — any conditions threatening the welfare of society were certain to encourage organized effort to change them for the better. So it was in the matter of drinking. In 1808 what is said to have been the first temperance society in the world was organized at Saratoga, New York. In the years that immediately followed the movement spread with some rapidity. A Massachusetts Society for the Suppression of Intemperance was formed in 1813, and in 1826 the American Society for the

Promotion of Temperance made its beginnings in Boston. Whether through the "suppression of intemperance" or the "promotion of temperance," it is recorded that by 1833 there were six thousand local societies scattered through several states, with a membership of more than a million. Up to this time the temperance campaign was directed chiefly against the use of spirituous liquors. In 1833 the American Society rejected the policy of seeking pledges of total abstinence, but reversed this action in 1836, when the "teetotal" principle, so-called from a local intensive term imported from northern England, was adopted.

It is worth noting at this point that Lincoln was not the first American President to identify himself publicly with the temperance movement. Witness a broadside, signed by three Presidents, and issued just over ninety years ago, while the reformers were still training most of their guns on "ardent spirits."

But of course the drift of sentiment was no more all in one direction then than it has been ever since. In 1838 the Massachusetts Legislature passed what was known as the "Fifteen-Gallon Law," a short-lived measure providing that spirituous liquors should not be sold "in a less quantity than fifteen gallons, and that delivered and carried away all at one time." A demand for its repeal soon presented by Harrison G. Otis "and Four Thousand Eight Hundred and Four others" was couched in terms clearly foreshadowing the expressions of our own contemporaries opposed to more recent liquor legislation. Indeed, the following expressions may stand to-day as a model of reasonable protest:

We ask them [the representatives of the people] not to compel those who have uniformly sustained the moral cause of temperance and still desire its success, to rally against this measure in defence of a higher principle than temperance itself, the liberty of the citizen. Very many of the devoted practical friends of temperance solemnly hold this law to be a violation of fundamental principles. They deny its right, they doubt its constitutionality, they are satisfied of its inexpediency, and that it will react, and retard the cause rather than advance it. They cannot consent to do wrong that good may possibly come. They will rather wait for moral causes to operate than force the end they wish to accomplish, at the expense of reaction and the soundest and plainest principles of equal rights.

While these agitations were proceeding in America, the first temperance organization in Europe was formed — where one would not quite have expected it — in the Irish town of Skibbereen. From this beginning in 1818, the movement spread through Ireland and into England. In Ireland the cause owed most of all to the eloquence of Father Mathew, a priest under whose influence it is declared that

Important Testimony!!

Nothing Sectarian or Political in the Temperance Cause.

The Chairman of the Executive Committee of the New York State Temperance Society, on his return from the great Temperance Convention, recently held in Virginia, obtained the following important testimony :

Being satisfied from observation and experience, as well as from Medical Testimony, that ardent spirit, as a drink, is not only needless, but hurtful; and that the entire disuse of it would tend to promote the health, the virtue, and happiness of the community, we hereby express our conviction, that would the Citizens of the United States, and especially all *Young Men*, discontinue the use of it, they would not only promote their own personal benefit, but the good of their country and the world.

(Signed,)   JAMES MADISON.
ANDREW JACKSON.
JOHN QUINCY ADAMS.

November, 1834.

A TEMPERANCE BROADSIDE SIGNED BY THREE PRESIDENTS OF THE UNITED STATES, 1834

from 1838 to 1842 nearly five millions of his countrymen — a number not far from the recent total
population of the island — became total abstainers
from liquor. From Ireland he carried his work as a
traveling speaker into England, and in 1850 to the
United States, where his name and appeal long survived in the many "Father Mathew Temperance
Societies" of the Roman Catholic Church. From
England as a boy in 1829, with his career of drink,
reformation, and temperance lecturing all before
him, came John B. Gough, regarded by a writer in
the *Police Gazette* as "just the man to produce a tem-
porary effect upon females or a mob," but by less
prejudiced observers as a flaming personal force in
the work for temperance.

Gough in his autobiography quoted the remark
of a Philadelphia lady: "We don't go to temperance
meetings; they are not genteel enough." And here,
as well as anywhere else, it is worth while to pause
for a moment, and consider what the remark im-
plies. It is indeed of no little significance. The cause
of temperance, from first to last, has paid the penalty of failing to enlist the support of those who set
the general fashions of living. Whatever savor of
smugness may be found in the fact — for such it
appears to be — that the example insisted upon
by Queen Victoria for her Court modified the

drinking-habits of English society at large, or in the words from an address, *The Drinking Usages of Society*, made by Bishop Alonzo Potter of Pennsylvania in 1852: "Fashion propagates itself downward," it has always been true in America as elsewhere, that those whose favored place in the world causes their conduct to fall under special scrutiny are responsible, with respect to drinking, for the conduct of many besides themselves. In this field of influence there is less need of missionaries to the Indians — figurative as well as literal — than to the Fashionables.

By the time Gough took the temperance platform in the early forties, the movement was under one of those full swings of enthusiasm which have alternated throughout its history with periods — shall I say? — of relapse. The fervor of the thirties is suggested in the humorless final stanza of a song for the Fourth of July meeting of the Philadelphia Mechanics' and Workingmen's Temperance Society in 1835:

> No, let us rise united,
>   And the great monster crush.
> By water draughts excited,
>   We to the rescue rush!

In a pamphlet of 1841, *The New Impulse, by a Teetotaler*, these even more exalted words are found:

JOHN B. GOUGH AND FATHER MATHEW

"Nothing in the world, since the appearance of our Saviour on earth, has produced such wonder and admiration as the recent conversion of a world of drunkards to one of sober life and conversation, and even to firm, resolute, persevering temperance reformers carrying all before them, leaving the old reformers and the world at large lost in amazement, inquiring, 'What do these things mean, and whence have these men their power?' "

These new reformers, so confidently acclaimed as "carrying all before them," were the participants in the "Washingtonian movement," which originated in Baltimore in 1840, at the initiative of a small group of reformed drunkards. It spread amazingly throughout the country. Local Washingtonian societies were organized here and there and everywhere, and some half-million persons, including many former drunkards, signed the pledge of total abstinence. But the efficacy of the movement was short-lived. Those who had counted upon it to regenerate mankind, at least in America, had not reckoned sufficiently on the backsliding propensities of individual human beings. Indeed the experience of nearly half a century was showing the more thoughtful reformers that real progress must proceed from something more permanent than the results from the recurrent revivals of temperance agitation. Accordingly the emphasis of temperance reform was shifted from the personal appeal to the legislative control of traffic in liquor. This found its first full expression in the Maine prohibition law, enacted under the leadership of General Neal Dow in 1851, and maintained, with varying degrees of success, until the national prohibition law superseded it. Before 1860 a dozen states had followed the Maine example, and by 1890 seventeen states in all had "gone dry," for longer and shorter periods of experiment. Between the authorities that made the laws and the individuals who drank the liquor there was one agency against which the temperance reformers came to direct their energies with steadily increasing vigor. That was the saloon.

In the full flower of its influence the saloon had few defenders outside the circle of its most devoted patrons and those "liquor interests" which fattened upon its profits. To the statistics of crime and vice it was making contributions of appalling significance. Such effects were fairly obvious and ponderable. The effect of the saloon upon politics grew even more disturbing, because it was comparatively imponderable. For a variety of reasons the saloon thus became the vulnerable point in the armor of defense against the temperance reformers.

For purposes of attack a dramatic gesture is often

of high value. Such a gesture appeared a little more than fifty years ago, in what was called "The Woman's Crusade." It began after this wise. In December 1873, Dr. Dio Lewis, a Boston lecturer on temperance and physical education, visited Fredonia and Jamestown, New York, Hillsboro and Washington Court House, Ohio, in each of which towns he led a number of women in the churches to deal with the local saloons by visiting them in bands to plead with the liquor-sellers to desist from their traffic, and, by means of hymns and prayers uttered on the spot, to invoke divine aid in their enterprise. Dr. Lewis's lecture in Hillsboro, a few days before Christmas 1873, seems to have been the most effective of all, for the demonstration of the women of that town on Christmas Eve, when they visited the drugstores and bars of the place, striking terror to the hearts of liquor-sellers by their hymns, prayers, and personal pleas, served as an example for the immediate formation of "praying bands" throughout Ohio, and as the direct forerunner of the organization of the Women's Christian Temperance Union at Cleveland in November 1874.

The movement was well named "The Woman's Crusade." A religious zeal, closely akin to that which quickened the Crusaders of the Middle Ages, animated the bands of devoted women, marching through rain and snow, singing the Crusade hymn, "Give to the winds thy fears," falling on their knees at and within the doors of saloons which they were wont to shun as plague-spots; pouring out their souls in prayer, and in an astonishing number of instances actually persuading the saloonkeepers to empty their bottles and barrels into the gutters. The attack, for the first time entirely feminine, was centred more completely than ever before upon the saloons, and with all that religious emotion of which the scoffers at the temperance movement, then and ever since, have failed to realize the unremitting driving power. It made no matter that one Ohio saloonkeeper, on the steps of whose "place" the women prayed for weeks, adorned his windows for a time — as many others must have wished to do — with the picture of a corpse on a bier, inscribed, "This man was talked to death." The crusade spread like a prairie fire. Long after the W.C.T.U. grew out of it a Southern chairman who introduced Miss Willard as the spokesman for the motto, "We come to unite," perceived the significance of the enterprise more clearly than the profane who have interpreted the initials as meaning "We see to you." Be that as it may, it was on the wave of the enthusiasm originating with the praying bands of Ohio and culminating in the Women's

Christian Temperance Union that Frances E. Willard came into the movement with which her name is indelibly identified.

II

Every cause has its pioneers and its later devotees — even the laborers of the eleventh hour — whose contribution to the ultimate object of all the workers may prove decisive. Frances Willard died about twenty years too soon to see the achievement of the two great ends to which she applied her extraordinary powers — national prohibition and woman suffrage, objects regarded by her as one and inseparable. But for nearly twenty-five years, ending with her death in 1898, they were the very breath of her being, and there can be no doubt that the lavish expenditure of her gifts of organization, of utterance through the spoken and written word, and of direct personal influence, all employed with enormous physical energy, bore a vital relation to the ultimate adoption of the Eighteenth and Nineteenth Amendments to the Constitution of the United States. Far-reaching changes in governmental policies, especially in matters of social import, come to pass in large measure through personal forces. It was Frances Willard's contribution to the cause of temperance — which to her meant prohibition — that she embodied, quite commandingly, the sentiment of women and the impulsion of religion, a formidable junction of powers. Any consideration of her character and career must illuminate two points, her immediate part in the temperance movement and the twin qualities of an effective reformer, absolute belief in a cause and, to an equal degree, in one's self.

For this confidence in herself Frances Willard had good ground. Through both her father, Josiah Flint Willard, and her mother, Mary Thompson (Hill) Willard, she inherited the sturdiest New England qualities of self-reliance. She liked to interpret the name Willard as meaning "one who wills," and did not reject its other definition, "will-hard." From her first American ancestor of the name, Major Simon Willard, a founder of Concord, Massachusetts, many distinguished persons, including two who occupied the president's chair at Harvard, traced their descent. Her mother's forbears were of New Hampshire and Vermont stock. A story of her Grandfather Hill suggests something of their quality. Long before the antislavery agitation began to affect men's minds, he employed as a farm hand in a sheep-shearing season a negro youth, the first of his color in the neighborhood. Like the other hands on the farm, he came to the family table for his meals, which led one of John Hill's daughters to make this appeal to her father: "Sister Abigail has a very poor appetite and cannot relish her food at the table with that colored man. Can he wait?" "No," replied the inexorable parent, "but she can."

In 1816 both the Willard and the Hill grandparents of Frances Willard moved across the snow from northern Vermont to western New York, and settled at Ogden, not far from Rochester. Two Willard sons married two Hill daughters, and on September 28, 1839, Frances Elizabeth Willard, who narrowly escaped receiving the name of Victoria in tribute to the young Queen, was born at Churchville, a few miles from Ogden. Two older sisters had died in childhood before her birth. One older brother, Oliver, was living. Before the birth of her sister Mary the family had moved to Oberlin, Ohio, where the father, well on in the thirties, took up collegiate studies in the hope of becoming a minister. But his physical strength proved unequal to the effort, and, in the spring of 1846, under orders to lead an outdoor life, he marshaled his family farther westward, traveling by prairie schooner, through Chicago in its quagmire stage, to the spot on the Rock River, near Janesville, Wisconsin, where they built their "Forest Home."

Here the Willard children — "Frank," as Frances

was habitually, perhaps not unmeaningly, called, her brother, and her sister — led a life that was calculated to bring out many qualities which would have passed unevoked in more conventional surroundings. The parents' genuine love of nature was transmitted to the children, and with it the love of books and of beauty. When the boy was allowed, before the girls, to ride a horse, "Frank" trained a cow to the saddle, and Mary fitted out a goat with panniers to carry food and drawing materials when they set forth to sketch. But art and piety had to be reconciled. The father of the family, who would not shave, black his boots, write a letter, or look up a word in the dictionary on the Sabbath, forbade all Sunday drawing. "May n't I have my new slate," Frances begged of her mother, "if I 'll promise not to draw anything but meetin'-houses?" And the mother wisely made her a picture to copy. Even her father, on a Sunday walk, relented when she begged, "But, father, can't I whittle, if I 'll promise that I won't *make* anything?"

It is hard to associate such rigors of one sort with such enthusiasms of another as parents and children alike displayed in their quest of a liberalizing education. All the facilities within reach, even as far away as Milwaukee, were seized. Mrs. Willard herself — Madam Willard and "Saint Courageous" she came to be called in her stately older age — had been a school-teacher in New York State before her marriage, and made the poets her companions through life. A woman of great good sense, in addition to uncommon force of character, she made reply in the Chicago suburb of Evanston — whither the Willard family had moved when their educational demand exceeded the local Wisconsin supply — to a lady's inquiry about the best means of culture in rural neighborhoods: "I should say, pack up your duds and go where folks live."

Before the Willards left Wisconsin Frances had revealed many qualities, including vigor, independence and self-confidence, which marked her through life. The tendency to organize and to pledge — herself and others — manifested itself early. To mitigate the loneliness of Forest Home it was suggested that the framework of a city, at least on paper, should be erected in the solitudes. "If we ought to have a city here, we will have one," said Frank, and proceeded to draw up an elaborate code of "Laws of Forest City." The "will-hard" tendency expressed itself thus in one provision of their "general laws": "If any person has seen or heard of a thing he wishes to have, he shall have it for all of any officer of this city: that is, after he has said, *I speak for that thing*, or something of that sort."

From her beloved sister Mary she exacted the signed pledge, "I, Mary Willard, promise never to touch anything lying or being upon Frank Willard's stand and writing-desk which father gave her" — to which many binding details were added. With her sister she formed, besides, a Rustic Club and an Artists' Club, with careful rules and regulations, of which the last, in the Artists' Club of two, read: "We, the members of this Club, pledge ourselves to keep faithfully all these our own laws." Still more to the point, in relation to her adult activities, was a total abstinence pledge pasted by Frank in the family Bible, for both parents and the three children, led by her, to sign. Its ten lines of verse began:

> A pledge we make, no wine to take,
> Nor brandy red that turns the head,

and ended:

> To quench our thirst we 'll always bring
> Cold water from the well or spring;
> So here we pledge perpetual hate
> To all that can intoxicate.

Linking the woman suffrage with the temperance influences of these early years, an incident of her childhood should be recalled in her own words:

Longer ago than I shall tell, my father returned one night to the far-off Wisconsin home where I was reared; sitting by

my mother's chair with a child's attentive ear, I listened to
their words. He told us of the news that day had brought
about Neal Dow and the great fight for prohibition down in
Maine, and then he said, "I wonder if poor rum-cursed Wisconsin will ever get a law like that?" And mother rocked a
while in silence in the dear old chair I love, and then she gently
said: "Yes, Josiah, there 'll be such a law all over the land
some day, when women vote."

It was in the spring of 1858 that the Willard
family moved from Wisconsin to Evanston, Illinois, then a new suburb of Chicago, in which devoted groups of Methodists had placed the Northwestern University, the Garrett Biblical Institute,
and the Northwestern Female College. The Willards had identified themselves heartily with the
Methodist Church in Wisconsin, and were drawn
to Evanston as a new and promising educational
centre of their denomination — the more promising
in their eyes because the sale of liquor within four
miles of the college campus was forbidden by the
charter of the University. Miss Willard described
the town on one page of her writings as "the Methodist Cambridge of the prairies," and elsewhere
wrote that it was expected to become "the Methodist Athens of the West." Neither similitude is
quite apt, for neither to the American Cambridge
— assuming that town to have been in her mind
— nor to the Athens of antiquity can the term

Methodist conceivably be applied. The New England reticence that curbs the personal expressiveness characteristic of Methodism operates in the one case, the Grecian principle of "nothing too much" in the other.

The religious atmosphere of Evanston in the fifties and sixties seems, at least to the more restrained view of later years, to have been charged with almost everything too much. It was tempered, to be sure, by the background of scholarship provided by three institutions of higher learning; but such agencies as the prayer meetings, class meetings, and recurrent revivals kept the spiritual faculties at a vibrant tension. The sincerity of it all is obvious enough to persons who have known to what extent a vital, if sometimes less exuberant, religious faith dominated the daily lives of many Americans of the older generation. It is only fair to add, however, than when Frances Willard wrote of a "cheery old local preacher" that "he talks the United States language in the Methodist dialect thereof," she was suggesting unconsciously a quality of Evanston itself and something of its contribution to her own make-up.

Evanston—which she came to love so well that in later life she used to say, "When I go home to Heaven, I wish to register from Evanston" — was

indeed a place made for the young Frances Willard.
In the schools she had attended before leaving Wisconsin both she and her sister had shown ability
and ambition. Some of her verses, written in profusion near Janesville, had been printed by editors
to whom she submitted them. On her eighteenth
birthday, having suffered and resented the year
before the "martyrdom of long dresses and hair done
up woman-fashion," she burst into verse:

> The clock has struck!
> O! heaven and earth, I 'm free!

and openly defied her father's ban upon all novel-
reading by refusing to put down a copy of *Ivanhoe*,
and declaring, "I am of age — I am now to do what
I think right, and to read this fine historical story
is, in my opinion, a right thing for me to do." She
had adopted vigorous views on the rights of women
to the ballot, and altogether brought with her to
Evanston the abilities and spirit which were sure
to make her a marked figure in the college community.

There she distinguished herself both as a student
and, apparently, as a ringleader in a little band
called the "Ne'er-do-weels." Her later proprieties
give a special piquancy to the stories of her appearance as a pirate, using bad language and smoking a

cigar, and of losing her temper and knocking down a fellow student — of her own sex — who ridiculed a red worsted hood that sorted ill with her red hair. This was in her unregenerate days, while she was still writing unblushingly in her journal such sentiments as, "I have an unconquerable aversion to intercourse with my superiors in position, age, or education"; and "O the glory of *knowing* always when you are right"; and, in a letter, "If I were to pray, I should say, if I were *candid*, 'Oh, God, if there be a God, save my soul, if I have a soul!'" Before she left college, however, she resolved her doubts, and having passed untouched through more than one season of revivals, declared herself, alone and unexpectedly, at a Sunday evening service in the Methodist Church, a believer, of her own motion, in the faith of her parents and teachers. From this, with an extending tolerance which led her later in life to pronounce the beatitude, "Blessed are the inclusive, for they shall be included," she never departed.

The formative years were not finished, but those that intervened before she took up her active work for temperance must be touched upon, though with little of detail. They were filled with enlarging experiences: in teaching, in an escape from matrimony, in deep bereavement, and in foreign travel.

As a school-teacher her work was done, with notable success, in Illinois, at Pittsburgh, and at Lima, New York. For the better part of a year she was engaged to be married to a young theological student, Charles H. Fowler, who afterwards became the president of Northwestern University and a bishop in the Methodist Church. Discovering in time that her feeling for him was not of the sort on which marriage should be based, she broke the engagement, and within a year was writing in her journal, "I am glad, heartily glad, that I did not perjure myself in 1862." It was in June of that year that the death of her sister Mary, a young woman of the greatest charm and promise, brought her face to face with an overpowering grief. Out of it proceeded her first book, *Nineteen Beautiful Years*, an adoring memoir of the sister whose words, on the last day of her life, "Tell everybody to be good," became, as it were, the marching orders for Frances Willard's life thenceforth. Only a few years later she wrote with discouragement of her own "prolix, vapid style," and overabundant in many particulars it certainly was. Yet the first book, for all its unrestraint, had qualities of sincerity and felicity out of which the writer she wished to be might, with a certain discipline, have been made.

After a second great bereavement — her father's

death in 1868, like her sister's, from consumption — a friend possessed of comfortable means did the best thing in the world for her by taking her abroad for two years of travel. The two young friends were indefatigable in self-improvement. They went to Egypt where Frank, about to climb the pyramid of Cheops, confessed to a characteristic "secret determination to reach the top before any of my comrades"— which she did. At Jerusalem she recorded triumphantly, "A day of unrivaled execution." In Paris she and her hostess, Miss Jackson, attended lectures at the Sorbonne, and — far from Evanston! — even visited the theatres. More reckless still, in countries that did not count water among the beverages, and under a doctor's orders, she relaxed her

> perpetual hate
> To all that can intoxicate,

and learned, by her own admission, to put water in her wine rather than wine in her water. In her *Glimpses of Fifty Years*, it is even recorded that, finding her plate at a London dinner-party surrounded by seven wineglasses, she did "not protest or abstain." The naïveté of the avowal, "Beyond a flushing of the cheek, an unwonted readiness at repartee, and an anticipation of the dinner-hour, unknown to me before or since, I came under no

thralldom," is altogether disarming. Who shall
say that this brief departure from the straitest path
did not make her a better reformer in the end?

Returning to America in 1870 and taking up life
in "Rest Cottage" at Evanston with her mother,
Frances Willard was tacking down a stair-carpet one
day when a professor's wife who was visiting the
house exclaimed, "Frank, I am amazed at you! Let
someone else tack down carpets, and do you take
charge of the new college." "Very well," answered
Frank; "I shall be glad to do so. I was only waiting
to be asked." Thereupon she was asked to under-
take the presidency of the Evanston College for
Ladies, and accepted the invitation. After two
years, in 1873, the College united with Northwestern University, in which Miss Willard became Dean
of Women and Professor of Æsthetics. Meanwhile
her former fiancé, Fowler, had become President of
the University, and in a sharp conflict of opinion
over a matter of administration she resigned her
deanship in June 1874, gave herself up to an angry
night of tears at the loss of her Adamless Eden, and
employing all her Christian fortitude, put her disappointment behind her and stood ready, without
resentment, for the next task. Her later explanation
of the matter was this: "Dr. Fowler, the president
of the institution, has the will of Napoleon. I have

the will of Queen Elizabeth. When an immovable body meets an indestructible object, something has to give way." It was just as well that she had not become Mrs. Fowler.

The case was not at all that Miss Willard gave up her work as a teacher to enter the temperance movement, but rather that she was most opportunely ripe for this new employment of her powers. At thirty-five she found herself out of a job — the very job for which she regarded herself best fitted. The impetuous red-haired girl, with more of personal charm than her consciousness of shortcomings would let her acknowledge, had become a woman with manifest qualifications for leadership. Study, travel, and many human relationships had enriched her mind and spirit. Her wise mother's advice to "enter every open door" was a maxim that really guided her conduct. She was filled with zeal to make the world a better place through her sharing in its affairs. When the temperance door opened, she responded to the appeal not only of her early influences but, perhaps, also of the fact, naturally unmentioned by herself, that, in an instance deeply involving her affections, the problem of intemperance presented itself in personal terms. She was very ambitious, and frankly fond of approbation. She had no hesitation in recording as her "chief beset-

ments" at the time of her conversion, "a speculative mind, a hasty temper, a too-ready tongue, and
the purpose to be a celebrated person"; or in writing
of herself: "I always wanted to react upon the world
about me to my utmost ounce of power; to be widely
known, loved, and believed in — the more widely
the better. Every life has its master passion; this
has been mine." Where it would have carried her
without the very real and restraining power which
she derived from her religious faith, it is impossible
to say. "I find no other talisman but prayer," she
once wrote, "suffices to hold a temper naturally so
quick as mine under control." Ambition, self-confidence, the inevitable egotism of the reformer, the
sense of responsibility, all curbed and directed by a
deep and genuine spirit of religion — these forces,
joined in Frances Willard, made her the power
she was.

There were tempting opportunities to go on teaching when Miss Willard's work at Northwestern
University came to an end in 1874. But by that
time the Woman's Crusade was in full play, and all
that Frances Willard heard of its character and
performance must have roused in her the war horse
that smelleth the battle afar off. It was a conflict
as much made for her in her maturity as Evanston
was in her girlhood. Passing through Pittsburgh

as she returned from an Eastern visit in September
1874, she participated in the pious raid of a "praying band" upon a local saloon. A Chicago temperance society elected her its president immediately
upon her reaching home. In November she helped
to organize the National Women's Christian Temperance Union in Cleveland, and was chosen its secretary. In a resolution written by her and adopted
by the convention, the plainly religious purpose of
the W.C.T.U. was defined:

Resolved, that, recognizing the fact that our cause is, and
will be combated by mighty, determined, and relentless forces,
we will, trusting in Him who is the Prince of Peace, meet argument with argument, misjudgment with patience, denuncia-
tion with kindness, and all our difficulties and dangers with
prayer.

Five years later, in 1879, she was elected president
of the organization, and held the post for nineteen
fruitful years, until her death in New York, February 17, 1898.

To narrate in any detail the achievements of Frances Willard in her leadership of the Women's Christian Temperance Union and its myriad wearers of
the White Ribbon would be quite beyond the scope
of this paper. If the preceding pages have shown
what manner of person she was, what she did with
her opportunities may easily be imagined. The girl

who bemoaned her lot in the Wisconsin wilds with the words, "I wonder if we shall ever know anything, see anybody, or go anywhere!" came to know and to see immeasurably beyond the common lot, and reckoned her travels, abroad and at home, as covering some two hundred and fifty thousand miles. As a temperance advocate she spoke in every city and town of the United States numbering more than ten thousand inhabitants and in most of those with five thousand. "During her years of active life," said Senator Cullom at the dedication of her statue in the Capitol at Washington, "she probably addressed a larger number of public audiences than any man or woman of her time." Everything was on the heroic scale of size. In the course of a year, she answered twenty thousand letters. The "Polyglot Petition for Home Protection" addressed "To the Governments of the World (Collectively and Severally)," calling for the suppression of "indulgence in alcohol and opium, and in other vices which disgrace our social life," received more than a million signatures, in fifty languages, and measured some five miles of mounted names. On the principle that "everything is not in the Temperance Reform, but the Temperance Reform should be in everything," she adopted what she called her "Do Everything Policy," and espoused all manner of reforms, denouncing tobacco along with drink, insisting on a common standard of morality for men and women, allying herself with the labor and woman suffrage movements. With respect to the last it should be remarked in passing that she once disavowed any sympathy with the women "so prejudiced that . . . they would not allow a male grasshopper to chirp on their lawn." She confessed that "next to a wish I had to be a saint some day I really would like to be a politician"; and when each of the established political parties refused in 1884 to insert a prohibition plank in its platform, she defied and outraged many of her fellow workers unwilling to follow their cause into the arena of politics, by throwing in her lot with the Prohibition party. If this seemed a forlorn hope, she was not wholly blinded by it when she wrote, "We have learned that, if prohibition does not always prohibit, neither does civilization always civilize, nor education educate, nor Christianity Christianize."

There was indeed an extraordinary profusion of energy in all her activities and relationships. When the National W.C.T.U., for which she had framed the watchword, "For God and Home and Native Land," was federated with the World's W.C.T.U., the motto, by the easiest of expansions, became

"For God and Home and Every Land." At the age of fifty, she undertook to write her *Glimpses of Fifty Years*, and produced in three weeks a book of seven hundred generous pages of print. The publishers — the Woman's Temperance Publication Association — explain in an introductory note that five hundred additional pages, "written rapidly and without calculating for the space required by this overplus of manuscript," had to be omitted. The wonder is that with this wholesale way of doing things Miss Willard, so eminently a public figure, could maintain in her private life so much of intimate affection for family and friends. With her remarkable mother, who died in 1892, there was a bond of deep and effectual sympathy. In the fields of kinship and of fellowship in interest there were many, chiefly women, with whom she stood on terms of mutual devotion. With Lady Henry Somerset, the leader of the women's temperance movement in England, she formed an absorbing friendship that contributed greatly to the happiness of her final years. The remark by a biographer of this friend, "Lady Henry learnt from Miss Willard how to organize her work; Miss Willard learnt from Lady Henry how to dress becomingly," leaves much to be said. In Miss Willard's private relationships, indeed, a clue to her public fame, and the reasons for it, may possibly be found.

The training of her early years had made for expressiveness, for ignoring the barriers of reserve which block the outgivings of many human beings and even choke the inner springs of thought and speech. For her the usual inhibitions did not appear even to exist, and much of her success, both in dealing with individuals and in addressing multitudes, certainly lay in the strongly personal flavor which characterized all her activities. In the vast audiences which assembled to hear her as one of the most eloquent of orators, the individual — if one may judge from the reported effect of her speaking — was never permitted to feel himself merged completely in the mass. Charged by a friend with possessing "a fatal versatility," and recognizing the truth that lay behind the words, Frances Willard nevertheless brought to the cause she led — the religious work of women for temperance — and to all the other reforms which seemed to her inseparable from this cause, a sincerity and a directing force which must be counted among the powerful agencies leading to the adoption of prohibition as a national policy.

III

Miss Willard's early desire to become a celebrated person was abundantly gratified. There is no more striking proof of this than that when the State of

Illinois might have taken Grant or Stephen A. Douglas or John A. Logan, or even Lincoln, had he not been set apart for unique honors, as the subject of one of the two statues representing the State in Statuary Hall at Washington, it chose Frances E. Willard, the only woman so chosen by any state. But the marble figure represents more than a person — it represents a far-reaching influence. This was exerted through manifold channels: publications, educational work in schools, effort affecting legislation, public meetings, individual endeavor in directions innumerable, all under the guidance of the national and world organizations of which Miss Willard was the head. The effect of all these influences on the public mind of America — outside the circles in which any dictation with regard to social and personal usages is regarded as impertinent — has been beyond calculation.

The religious women could hardly have accomplished their self-appointed task alone. In 1895 the Anti-Saloon League began its increasingly aggressive warfare against what has already been described as the most vulnerable point of attack by temperance reformers — the saloon. Other influences came into play. In the South it was felt that the large, excitable Negro element of the population would be better without any legalized traffic in liquor, and many Southern States adopted prohibition. In the industrial world there was a spreading conviction that the efficiency of labor — with benefit both to itself and to capital — would increase under prohibitory laws. In the cities the growing army of social workers, observing at close range the worst effects of liquor on women and children, favored in general the cause of prohibition. Then came the war, with its exaltations and its revelations. "Jawn Barleycorn," wrote Mr. Dooley, "might have gone on f'r years if it had n't been that th' wurruld begun to suspect that he was no good in a fight. ... People said about him, 'He's a scamp and a false friend, but he's a divvle in a scrap.' An' now they know he ain't anny good at ayether. His bluff has been called." A war prohibition measure was adopted ten days after the signing of the Armistice, and came into effect June 30, 1919. Meanwhile the Eighteenth Amendment received the ratification of thirty-six states by January 16, 1919, and was officially proclaimed on January 30. On October 28, 1919, the Volstead Act was passed, over President Wilson's veto.

These laws and their operation are not the subjects of this chapter, which set out to deal, historically and biographically, with the temperance movement in general and one of its chief exponents

STATUE OF FRANCES E. WILLARD BY HELEN
FARNSWORTH MEARS IN STATUARY HALL,
NATIONAL CAPITOL, WASHINGTON

in particular. But there the laws are — the charter
of a vast experiment which the nation, by duly
appointed constitutional processes, after much preliminary trial and discussion, decided to make.
Whatever may befall the Volstead Act or even the
Eighteenth Amendment, one thing seems clear. For
the individual who subscribes to the democratic
principle of government by majorities the logical
and straightforward course is to refrain, even at
some personal and social inconvenience, from all
participation in the illegal traffic in liquor, to
expect of the naturally law-abiding classes that
they will leave the breaking of law to the naturally
law-breaking classes, and, if and when the national
experiment, after fair trial, proves a hopeless failure, to seek a new experiment at the hands of those
who have kept the democratic faith. Those who
cannot see the matter in this light — as many
sincere men and women in this particular instance
cannot — will do well to remember the force and
extent of prohibition sentiment throughout the
country before the existing national laws were
enacted, and especially to reckon with the legacy
of feeling which had its first and most startling
expression in the "praying bands" of Ohio and
the most eminent champion in that happy warrior,
Miss Willard.

In the early days of the long fight there were those on the one hand who advocated "moral suasion," and on the other, "legal suasion." Moral suasion was found inadequate. Now we have legal suasion, and its adequacy is still in grave question. Is it time again for moral suasion, on behalf of the common good, as affected both by the use of alcohol and by respect for the government and its laws? After all, any national way of life reflects a national sentiment, and that is the sum of individual feeling. Here then, is an issue — still an issue — from which no individual can escape.

IV

THE NEW USES OF GREAT WEALTH

PARTICULARLY BY THE ROCKEFELLERS

> O, IT is excellent
> To have a giant's strength; but it is tyrannous
> To use it like a giant.

MANY years ago these familiar words fixed themselves in my memory through their application, in
the ruthless irony of youth, to a college contemporary most feebly endowed with physical powers.
Now they come back as applicable to the industrial
dynasts of America, so multiplied in numbers
through recent decades, so variously employing
their "giant's strength," and so often employing
it for purposes other than tyrannous.

Only in the past fifty out of the approximately
three hundred years of American history has it been
possible to put great wealth to its new uses, for the
simple reason that, in the present meaning of the
term, it did not exist. Fifty years ago, indeed, it
was only beginning to foreshadow what it means
to-day, for it was not until the industrial development following the Civil War got into its full swing

that vast fortunes began to accumulate in private hands, and individuals had to ask themselves what in the world they could do with their embarrassing riches. Even before the time of Mr. John D. Rockefeller, Sr., others must have found themselves in the dilemma he recognized when he wrote:

These rich men we read about in the newspapers cannot get personal returns beyond a well-defined limit for their expenditures. They cannot gratify the pleasures of the palate beyond very moderate bounds, since they cannot purchase a good digestion; they cannot lavish very much money on fine raiment for themselves or their families without suffering from public ridicule; and in their homes they cannot go much beyond the comforts of the less wealthy without involving them in more pain than pleasure. As I study wealthy men, I can see but one way in which they can secure a real equivalent for money spent, and that is to cultivate a taste for giving where the money may produce an effect which will be a lasting gratification.

The conspicuous American precedents for securing this lasting gratification from private benefactions are found in the field of education. With all its limitations, Girard College in Philadelphia, admitting only white male orphans between six and ten, and as carefully excluding, even as visitors, all ecclesiastics, missionaries, and ministers of whatever sect, represented, before the Civil War, the effort of Stephen Girard, the most successfully self-made merchant of his time, to serve the public through education in its earlier stages. In its higher stages the cause of education has been served, incessantly from the beginning, by the gifts of individuals to the older endowed schools and colleges. No sooner was the Civil War behind us than three great new institutions of learning sprang into being through the generosity of individuals: Cornell University in 1865; Lehigh University in 1866; Johns Hopkins University in 1867. Meanwhile the marked increase in the number of state universities through the operations of the "Land Grant" Act of 1862 did not diminish the flow of individual private benefactions to the existing endowed colleges or discourage the establishment of new institutions. As wealth increased, it was perhaps most of all through an extension of the old American tradition of giving to the cause of education that its expenditure for the general good took form.

But the fortunes at the command of the donors of fifty years ago, magnificently large as their gifts then seemed, were small affairs in comparison with later accumulations. As the country grew and its industries developed, — especially through the geometric progression of combined industrial units, — the rewards for the type of ability which formed the units and engineered their combination began to exceed anything previously imagined. If these rewards have sometimes been used for futile purposes of ostentation, self-aggrandizement, gratification of the senses, and the exercise of personal power, there is surely no occasion for surprise. The pursuit of happiness takes many forms, varying widely in wisdom and efficacy. The reassuring thing is that in so very considerable a number of instances, a sense of stewardship, of holding in trust a power to confer enormous benefits, both immediate and distant, upon mankind has been a dominating impulse in the industrially dynastic families of the United States.

The results of action upon this impulse have appreciably affected American life. It may therefore be profitable to look at a few conspicuous instances of the voluntary employment of great wealth for the common good, and, in order to escape from an array of generalities into a concrete illustration of their drift, to consider the benefactions with which the name of Rockefeller is associated.

I

In looking at even an abridged list of the great private benefactions of recent years, the regularity with which a profitable industry relates itself in turn to each benefaction cannot escape notice. The fortune of Andrew Carnegie, still employed in furthering the causes of libraries, the teaching profession, education itself, and international peace, brings instantly to mind the word "steel." With the name of Carnegie also is linked the idea that to die rich and to die disgraced are synonymous terms, and the effect of this widely quoted sentiment has doubtless been considerable. Through Mrs. Russell Sage her husband's name, associated in his lifetime with railroad finance, is perpetuated in the Russell Sage Foundation for "the improvement of social and living conditions in the United States of America." Look at the evidences of Mr. George Eastman's contributions to the support of music and education, in and out of his own city of Rochester, New York, and the Kodak camera, which enabled him to do what he has done, will help you to carry away pictures of it all. In oil may be found not only the origin of the Rockefeller benefactions but also of the Commonwealth Fund, established for purposes of manifold helpfulness in social and educational fields by Mrs. Stephen V. Harkness. So it proceeds through many American sources of wealth. In England the *Dictionary of National Biography*, a publishing enterprise of the greatest magnitude and value, holds a high place among nineteenth-century contributions to the riches of a

people. How many of those who use it, wherever
the English language is spoken, realize that it had
its origin in the fortune acquired by George Smith,
of the firm of Smith and Elder, through his owner-
ship of the bubbling springs which fill the bottles
of Apollinaris water? From physical resources,
both solid and liquid, the resources of mind and
spirit derive their constant enrichment.

Directly or indirectly the cause of education is
represented in all the instances that have been cited.
Walk through the college grounds that beautify
our entire country, and in hall after hall you will
find a donor's name which may be identified with
an important industrial or commercial success. In
the college endowment funds and the countless in-
conspicuous ways in which an alumnus may serve
his alma mater, prosperity in one practical direction or another is expressed in smaller gifts. "This
is not wealth," said Andrew Carnegie of the accumulation of moderate sums, "but only competence,
which it should be the aim of all to acquire."
It was upon the smaller class to which he himself
belonged that he pronounced his familiar dictum:
"The day is not far distant when the man who dies
leaving behind him millions of available wealth,
which was free for him to administer during life,
will pass away 'unwept, unhonored, and unsung,'

no matter to what uses he leaves the dross which he cannot take with him. Of such as these the public verdict will then be: 'The man who dies thus rich dies disgraced.' " This is the man, granting him the best intentions in the world, who must think hard and straight before he can be perfectly sure — if indeed such certainty is ever possible — that in distributing from his abundance he will not do harm as well as good.

In a book, *Random Reminiscences of Men and Events*, which the older Mr. John D. Rockefeller published in 1909, he devotes one chapter to "The Difficult Art of Getting," and another to "The Difficult Art of Giving." He is an authority on both of these arts, and there is nothing to suggest that he regards one as more difficult than the other. The precedents for going wrong in the art of giving are many in number, ancient and modern. As far away as in imperial Rome, there was the *annona civica* (civic rations), which resulted in establishing the hereditary right in certain families to relief from the public funds. The endowments for obsolete objects of charity in England, including lepers, are embarrassingly frequent. Here in America the wise Ben Franklin created what seemed in his lifetime a generous and well-devised fund for the benefit of apprentices a century later — when apprentices had ceased to exist. A mayor of St. Louis in 1857 willed a considerable sum, now amounting to nearly a million dollars, to the relief of "worthy and distressed travelers and emigrants" on their way to establish bona fide homes in the West. It never occurred to him that St. Louis would change from a terminus to a way-station. And in Pennsylvania there was the woman who left an estate and $100,000 "to establish a home for superannuated Presbyterian clergymen above the age of seventy who do not use tobacco." It was held at first that the wives of these blameless gentlemen could not be admitted to the home, but when its occupants dwindled to one a court ruling lifted the embargo on both wives and weed. It is no wonder that public sentiment in recent years has favored the extension of the Community Trust idea, embodied only a little more than ten years ago in the Cleveland Foundation and already operative in about fifty American cities, under a carefully devised plan for devoting the income from benevolent trusts to the changing needs of mankind. But that is a story by itself — a different story from that of the largest foundations established by individuals.

In these the penalties of going wrong are even more serious than in the disposition of moderate fortunes. Because Mr. Rockefeller has justified his faith that "the same energy and thought should be expended in the proper and effective use of money when acquired as was exerted in the earning of it," because he has seen the realization of the hope he has "always indulged . . . that during my life I should be able to help establish efficiency in giving so that wealth may be of greater use to the present and future generations," his work in these directions is chosen for special scrutiny. He and his son — now more actively engaged in the execution of plans inherited, so to speak, from his father — are to-day the chief exponents of the "difficult art" of applying the highest intelligence to the useful expenditure of wealth almost unlimited. Representing thus what is virtually a new thing in the world, they and the facts about both their getting and their giving are legitimate objects not of vulgar curiosity, but of such study as may throw light upon the connection between the personal impulsion committing them to the cause for which they stand and its astonishing operations.

II

When John D. Rockefeller at the age of nineteen entered upon an independent business career as one of two partners in a firm of commission dealers in miscellaneous produce, the business success that lay ahead of him was predictable on one ground only — namely that the Sunday School and copybook maxims are all true. It would have been hazardous to base a prophecy upon them at the time, and indeed a prophecy of any success commensurate with his in store for other young men similarly situated would almost certainly have failed of fulfillment. In outward circumstances many others have been confronted with the same valuable opportunities in the form of handicaps to be overcome. The unpredictable thing is something internal, not external, and that is what John D. Rockefeller possessed.

The maxims are nevertheless verified in important particulars. The spirit of thrift and the spirit of religion — especially that workaday form of religion that manifests itself in sharing one's possessions, whether large or small, with others — were bred in him from infancy by parents who believed, honestly and completely, in these elements of happy and useful living. Born in Richford, Tioga County, New York, July 8, 1839, he was primarily fortunate in his parents. His father, William Avery Rockefeller, presumably of Huguenot and certainly of Yankee descent, was a physician and business man of energy, thrift, and piety. His mother, Eliza (Davison) Rockefeller, combined a strong religious

faith with a stern sense of discipline. Mr. Rockefeller himself tells of a whipping he received from
her for an offense of which he protested his inno-
cence. "Never mind," said his mother, "we have
started in on this whipping, and it will do for next
time." The "next time" was reasonably sure to
come at the hands of parents who could not condone
the disobedience of their sons, John and William, in
skating on a moonlight night, even though this
breaking of a family rule resulted in the saving of a
neighbor's life. It was an old-fashioned bringing-
up, but with precept backed by example. The
father's business standards were reflected in those of
his son John, who learned lessons of finance from
early experiments as a farm boy in raising turkeys
and digging potatoes.

When he was fourteen the Rockefeller family
moved to Cleveland, and the boy began to keep a
little account book, now proudly preserved and
designated "Ledger A." It records his first meagre
earnings of fifty dollars for three months of service
at the end of 1855 as an assistant bookkeeper in a
forwarding and commission house, and an advance
to twenty-five dollars a month at the beginning of
1856. Then in a year came an annual salary of $500,
followed by an offer of $700, which the young clerk
refused because he thought he was worth eight.

But he had already begun to save, and through borrowing $1000 from his father at the current rate of ten per cent was able to join in 1858 with a young Englishman, Morris B. Clark, in establishing the commission house of Clark and Rockefeller.

But Ledger A is as significant on the "giving" as on the "getting" side. It shows, for example, the systematic giving of one cent a week to the Sunday School in the days of scantiest income. In the five months from November 1855 to April 1856 it appears that young Rockefeller gave away in all $5.58. When he was nearing sixty he summarized these revelations of Ledger A in saying: "In one month I gave to foreign missions, ten cents; to the Mite Society, fifty cents, and there is also a contribution to the Five Points Mission. I was not living then in New York, but I suppose that I felt that it was in need of help, so I sent up twelve cents to the mission. Then to the venerable teacher of my class I gave thirty-five cents to make him a present. To the poor people of the church I gave ten cents at this time, and in January and February following I gave ten cents more, and a further ten cents to the foreign mission."

These items would be quite unimportant but for their illustration of a principle stated by Mr. Rockefeller himself: "It is a mistake for a man who wishes for happiness and to help others to think that he will wait until he has a fortune before giving away money to deserving objects." Another article of his creed appears in the same discussion of Ledger A: "I believe it is a religious duty to get all the money you can, fairly and honestly; to keep all you can, and to give away all you can."

This identification of religious and financial duty is illustrated by the fact that when Mr. Rockefeller describes the part he bore in collecting funds to pay off the mortgage on a Baptist mission church in Cleveland, at about the time of his election at seventeen or eighteen as one of its trustees, he declares: "My first ambition to earn more money was aroused by this and similar undertakings in which I was constantly engaged." Nor was his work for his church by any means confined to money-raising. For many years — the very years in which he was building up his fortune — he served as superintendent of the Sunday School of the Euclid Avenue Baptist Church. It was a Cleveland friend and neighbor who wrote of him at this time: "From the first he has won the love of the children from his sympathy, kindness, and his interest in their welfare. No picnic ever would be satisfactory to them without his presence."

Fortunately there is no necessity of reconciling

the apparent discrepancies between such a person as this gentle "life of the party" and the powerfully malign figure who stalks through the pages of Miss Ida M. Tarbell's *History of the Standard Oil Company* (1904). History is full of these contradictions, and Miss Tarbell's book, written in the palmiest days of the "muck-raking" period, strikes a dispassionate reader of twenty years later as primarily a document in the interest of the independent producers of oil. You can read the other side of the story in Gilbert Holland Montague's book, *The Rise and Progress of the Standard Oil Company* (1903), in which the case for this organization is presented with perhaps an equally obvious bias in its favor. Or you can read Mr. Rockefeller's own *Random Reminiscences of Men and Events* (1909), which caused "Mr. Dooley" to remark: "There's wan thing sure fr'm what I can see, an' that is that Jawn D. hasn't an idea that he iver did wrong to annywan. I like that about him; it shows he's a human being."

The historian will read all these books, and from the last of them will at least derive some understanding of what the great painter, John S. Sargent, meant when, after spending some weeks in close relations with Mr. Rockefeller, he said that he felt as if he had been in the company of a mediæval saint. Another artist, Mr. Jo Davidson, spent some days of June 1924 with Mr. Rockefeller at his home on the Hudson, making a portrait bust. He confirms both Mr. Dooley and the appreciative painter by saying that Mr. Rockefeller struck him as the most patient man he ever met, and seemed sure that he had always done the right thing. But he could see shadows in the old man's face, and quotes him as saying one evening, "You know, for years I was crucified. It is better now."

The *Random Reminiscences* indeed produce a clear effect of sincerity, simplicity, and unselfishness. This of course is not the impression produced by Miss Tarbell and reflected in public opinion as expressed in the press of twenty and fifteen years ago. A significant test of this feeling may be found by looking, in the *Readers' Guide to Periodical Literature*, at the titles of magazine articles published through several years beginning about 1905 on the subject of the Rockefeller benefactions, then beginning to occupy a conspicuous place in public interest. Throughout the list of these articles, the "tainted money" aspect of their topic — an aspect from which the emphasis was gradually removed until it has quite disappeared — was markedly prominent. The image of the Standard Oil Company, uniting in 1870 the oil interests with which Mr.

Rockefeller began to identify himself in 1865, and grown at the beginning of the present century to an unexampled stature of wealth and power, was still the image of a ruthless monster, bitted and reined by an equally ruthless man. In a world of competition neither man nor organization can become supremely successful without leaving beside the pathway of advance a broken line of defeated figures, suffering from wrongs either real or imaginary or both. "The Lord God Himself could not make room for the great without narrowing the range of the small." So speaks John D. Rockefeller in a fictitious colloquy with Tolstoi, invented by Maximilian Harden before the war. "And," the imaginary Rockefeller proceeds, "because I have done this, enriched my country, done service to millions, helped whole races to the light, and led thousands to the loftiest sources of culture, I, a sinner stained with all the vices of industrious creative work, set my life achievement higher than that of a fruitlessly holy man." There are indeed many ways of looking at it all.

It is not the function of this article to analyze and pronounce upon the processes by which the Rockefeller fortune was accumulated; that would be to discuss the entire economic system in which the Standard Oil Company has represented the outstand-

JOHN D. ROCKEFELLER, JO DAVIDSON, SCULPTOR, AND HIS WORK, JUNE 1924

ing instance of successful achievement. What should be said here is that the success has been due in largest measure to the combination of far-searching vision and intense application to detail on the part of one man equipped in unique degree with what obviously amounts to genius in the handling of industrial, commercial, and financial problems, and playing the great game of business, on a colossal scale, according to the ethical rules of the game as they stood at the time when he and his shrewdly chosen associates were laying the foundations on which the structure of their success has reared its towering head. This is the same man, always cool, with an unvarying pulse of slow beat, addicted through life to the simplest personal habits, who began, at the very beginning of his reaping the rewards of his own industry, slender as they were at first, to share systematically with others what he was able to save. "As my father taught me," he wrote, "so I have tried to teach my children" — with the result that, in contrast with the paupered families of ancient Rome, in which the *annona civica* bred an hereditary right to relief, there has been bred in this family an hereditary right to relieve. It is, again, the man of whom his son could write about ten years ago: "Criticized, maligned, and condemned these many years, not only for his business success achieved through his ability to gain the confidence and coöperation of men, to bring all parties into harmony, and to effect economies in every possible way, but also because of his philanthropic endeavors, there is still not the slightest trace of bitterness in his character and he holds in his heart nothing but good will toward every man."

John D. Rockefeller, Sr., is now in his eighty-eighth year, John D. Rockefeller, Jr., in his fifty-third. It is a new world in which the younger man has grown up. If the older has come to look on many things in a new light, that is the light to which the changes in social, industrial, and religious conditions in America have accustomed the younger man ever since he began to assume his enormous responsibilities. In the form of wealth and of the powers, excellent or tyrannous, which it enables its possessor to exercise, these responsibilities now rest primarily upon him. He has been called "a new kind of millionaire," and the definition is apt, for, finding himself in control of resources which from their very abundance attach to the word "money" an entirely unfamiliar meaning, he has made it his chief concern to see that they shall be used to the greatest possible advantage of his fellow creatures. The new world in which he

JOHN D. ROCKEFELLER, FATHER AND SON

is living is notorious for the chasm between the older and younger generations. Many of the old sanctions and safeguards of existence are believed to have disappeared. The spectacle of the Rockefellers, father and son, contradicts this belief. The essentials of a strong religious faith, with the Christian grace of giving at its core, have obviously been transmitted from the one to the other. Now for about thirty years the son has been in the closest contact with both the business affairs and the benefactions of the father. They have both been Sunday School teachers, to the confusion of those with a different standard of relative values; they have both made incalculable contributions to the development of American industry. The one instituted, the other is actively concerned with, the benevolent trusts that bear their name; and it is time to see how the principles of efficiency employed in the art of getting are now applied in that of giving.

III

In the systematic offerings of pennies and dimes to the causes in which the older Mr. Rockefeller was brought up to believe, it has already been seen that the principle of his benefactions was founded. The successive steps in the growth of his giving are not to be followed. They would doubtless be found first to lie chiefly, and quite naturally, in the direction of Baptist denominational objects. In the early eighties, when the Standard Oil Company had been in existence only a little more than ten years, Mr. Rockefeller became a vice-president of the Baptist Theological Union of Chicago, and soon began to give financial support to the Baptist Union Theological Seminary in that city, an institution with which Dr. W. R. Harper, afterwards president of the University of Chicago, had become associated in 1879. In 1886 a prematurely born University of Chicago gave up the struggle it had waged, under Baptist auspices, against Civil War conditions, "the fire," and debt. Those who believed that a great future lay beyond its possible revival were already in contact with Mr. Rockefeller through their common interest in the Baptist Union Theological Seminary.

In 1888 the American Baptist Education Society came into being, with the Rev. Frederick T. Gates as its executive secretary. One of the first objects of the Society was to establish a thoroughly equipped Baptist institution of learning in Chicago. Dr. Harper had already impressed himself upon Mr. Rockefeller as a man of extraordinary power. Mr. Gates — to whom Mr. Rockefeller some twenty years later ascribed "a combination of rare business

ability, very highly developed and very honorably
exercised, overshadowed by a passion to accomplish some great and far-reaching benefits to mankind, the influence of which will last" — made it
his immediate object to interest Mr. Rockefeller in
the project of the great University, of which the
Baptist Union Theological Seminary was eventually to become the Divinity School. In 1889 Mr.
Rockefeller pledged the sum of $600,000 towards
the establishment of the University of Chicago, on
the condition that $400,000 should be raised from
other sources. Continuing for about thirty years,
his gifts to this University have amounted to approximately $35,000,000. It is not surprising that
the trustees as early as 1890 adopted a seal inscribed:
*Sigillum Universitatis Chicaginiensis A. D. MDCCCXC
A Johanne Davison Rockefeller Fundatae;* or that the
students expressed themselves, less classically, in a
"yell" which was improvised for the quinquennial
celebration in 1896, and — to the credit of undergraduate taste — has not endured:

> Who's the feller? Who's the feller? Rah, Rah, Rah!
> Rockefeller, he's the feller, Sis! Boom! Ah!

Such gifts to the cause of higher education as Mr.
Rockefeller thus began making many years ago are
in themselves highly educative, particularly when

the giver himself, bent on the fullest "efficiency in giving," brings a keen and trained intelligence to bear on the objects to be helped and the best possible means of helping them. Like every successful man of affairs, Mr. Rockefeller has owed much of his success to the skill with which he has picked his associates and organized their efforts. With the expansion of his resources and of their distribution, what amounted to an office staff for purposes of benevolence came into existence at the New York headquarters of his business, more associated, in the public mind, with getting than with giving. Both in the execution and in the planning of his work — as in such purely business matters as the building and management of ore steamers on the Great Lakes — Mr. Gates, known first to Mr. Rockefeller as a minister and officer of the American Baptist Education Society, proved himself extremely useful and far-seeing.

Until the full personal story of it all can be told the development of the present scheme for distributing vast and steadily increasing funds cannot be followed in detail. Certain principles, however, must have become clear to Mr. Rockefeller and his advisers as early as the eighties, when the gifts to the University of Chicago began. Among them were the careful preliminary study of the object to be helped, that there may be no doubt of its worthiness; the giving of a portion rather than the whole of the sum desired for this object, that others may be stimulated to a contributory and continuing interest in it; and the policy, after giving to an object of proved value, of trusting the expenditure of the sums so bestowed entirely to those who are responsible for the institution or cause that has been helped. These indeed are underlying principles in all the Rockefeller benefactions.

Another important point of policy, followed by the boards in their corporate capacity, has been the avoidance of objects, social, political, religious, of which the influence upon the public is in any way open to question. The causes of general education and general health are obviously causes from which an entire people may expect to profit. Yet, says the Annual Report of the Rockefeller Foundation for 1917 in terms which may be taken as an official interpretation of the Rockefeller principle of corporate giving, there are things which a Foundation "cannot successfully or wisely do; such as, for example, give money or make loans to individuals, or invest in securities which have a philanthropic rather than a business basis, or assist in securing patents, or aid altruistic movements which involve private profit. It must also refrain from supporting propaganda which seek to influence public opinion about the social order, and political proposals, however disinterested and important these may be. Thus, appeals to finance in whole or in part a speakers' bureau in behalf of the war, the teaching of patriotism in the public schools, and an advertising campaign for national prohibition have been denied on principle."

In the general fields of health and education let us then see what the benevolent trusts established by Mr. Rockefeller were designed to accomplish and are accomplishing. The Rockefeller Institute of Medical Research, founded in 1901, was the first of the existing bodies to be organized. Its purpose, as defined in its charter from the State of New York, is:

To conduct, assist, and encourage investigations in the sciences and arts of hygiene, medicine, and surgery, and allied subjects, in the nature and causes of disease and the methods of its prevention and treatment, and to make knowledge relating to these various subjects available for the protection of the health of the public and the improved treatment of disease and injury. [These ends are sought, under a Board of Trustees and a Board of Scientific Directors, by various means] including research, publication, education, the establishment and maintenance of charitable or benevolent activities, agencies, or institutions appropriate thereto, and the aid of any other such activities, agencies, or institutions already established or which may hereafter be established.

Here indeed is what is known as a "large order."
Believing strongly in the fundamental value of such
an enterprise, Mr. Rockefeller first committed himself to it only to the extent of pledging to its support the sum of $200,000, payable in ten annual
installments of $20,000. With no more definite
assurance than this, the men of science who began
to work at the Institute bore notable witness in so
doing to their faith in its purposes. At first it was
thought that the ends in view could be attained by
sustaining research work in one or more existing
institutions or private laboratories. As time went
on, the advantages of assembling all the workers in
New York for the sake both of natural stimulus
and of profiting by the wealth of experimentative
material in a great centre of population became
more apparent. To meet these possibilities, Mr.
Rockefeller steadily enlarged the resources of the
Institute, so that it now occupies spacious labora-
tory and hospital buildings of its own, overlooking
the East River in New York City, and has established a Department of Animal Pathology in lab-
oratory and animal buildings at Princeton, New
Jersey.

The beneficent work of the Institute in many
fields of medical research, the results of which are
all available for general use, cannot be summarized

in a few words. High among the triumphs are the discoveries of a curative serum for epidemic cerebrospinal meningitis, of another for one of the fatal forms of pneumonia, and the study of infantile paralysis which yielded the microbe causing the disease and, by uncovering the way that germ enters the human body, pointed to a means of prevention. For further practical advances in the prevention and cure of disease, there have been fundamental inquiries in the fields of biology, chemistry, and physics, and successful efforts to control diseases of economic animals on which certain food supplies of man depend. During the World War a War Demonstration Hospital was erected on the grounds of the Institute for Dr. Carrel. Here many surgeons who afterwards served in France were trained by him in the treatment of infected wounds. The so-called Carrel-Dakin method of treating infected wounds, perfected by Dr. Carrel and Dr. Dakin, was not only employed with signal success during the war, but is now established as one of the trustworthy means of combating wound infection in ordinary hospital practice.

In illustration of Mr. Rockefeller's vastly greater interest in results than in any of the machinery by which they are reached, a significant story may be told. It is to the effect that his son, long desirous of causing the father to see and enter the buildings of the Institute, — which he had never done, — beguiled him one day in a cab from Park Avenue, where they had stood together on the sidewalk eagerly discussing a matter of common interest, to East 66th Street and Avenue A. The elder Mr. Rockefeller was still talking of the subject uppermost in his mind when they alighted in the new quarter. Again they stood on the sidewalk talking, the son trying in vain even to call his father's attention to the buildings which rose before them. The time for keeping an engagement elsewhere drew near, and, abandoning his effort as hopeless, the son took his seat again in the cab beside his father, and they drove away — the Rockefeller Institute as a physical fact still unregarded by its founder. Bring him, however, a new discovery from the Institute, and nobody can be more keen to hear all about it.

A year after the establishment of the Rockefeller Institute for Medical Research the organization of the General Education Board was planned. Incorporated by an Act of Congress on January 19, 1903, it took for its object, as defined in its charter, "the promotion of education within the United States, without distinction of race, sex, or creed," and was authorized to pursue these ends by a great variety of means. In an early report by the Secretary of the Board, the general principles underlying its work are set forth in terms that throw a clear light upon the spirit in which the Rockefeller benefactions as a whole are conducted. In brief, a careful investigation is first required, to prove that an institution which may be helped is necessary, reasonably well located, and likely to be permanent. These points established, "the Board may make a contribution to a fund, the raising of which has already been determined." The contribution is made to permanent endowment, not for building, grounds, or apparatus, and not for the support of particular academic departments, chairs, or lines of work, in which such a gift might affect the internal policy of the institution, and frustrate a quick response in changed conditions.

But it would be quite misleading to give the impression that the help of existing institutions is the only, or even the chief, activity of the Board. Mr. Rockefeller's first gift to the endowment — $10,000,000 — was designed to support an inquiry into the educational needs of the Southern people. It is a significant fact that the Board recognized the need of a better economic condition in the South before it would be possible to support an adequate school system, as it should be supported, by local taxation. Accordingly an educational campaign of "farm demonstrations" was undertaken, and state, national, and county authorities have coöperated in it to the lasting advantage of large agricultural districts. Yet this has been only one of a number of activities, summarized thus:

(1) The promotion of practical farming in the Southern States; (2) coöperation with state universities in the development of a system of public night schools, rural schools, and schools for Negroes in the Southern States; (3) the promotion of higher education throughout the United States; (4) development of university medical departments; (5) encouragement of educational research and investigation.

Again a large order. Even to suggest in any detail how it has been filled is impossible in a limited space. It should, however, be recorded that successive gifts of Mr. Rockefeller to the General Education Board have brought the $10,000,000 of its original resources to nearly $130,000,000, now reduced to something less than $80,000,000 through the exercise of the Board's power to apply both interest and principal to the objects of its help. This method of distribution is in literal fulfillment of Mr. Rockefeller's own purposes. When he gave some $20,000,000 to the Board in 1919 for the advancement of medical education in the United States his words about it were, "the income to be used currently and the principal to be expended within the next fifty years." Of itself the Board has said in one of its annual reports: "In due time, its objects will have been achieved, and problems will have emerged. The General Education Board will then have ceased to exist. The statesmen and benefactors of the next age will invent the organizations and provide the means then requisite."

Without waiting for the next age to arrive, it became evident in a little more than ten years that, beyond advanced researches in the field of medical science and beyond the furthering of education in America only, there were important objects to be helped which could be helped in accordance with the general Rockefeller plan of assistance; that into other outlets a fresh flow of support might be poured. Therefore to the Rockefeller Institute for Medical Research and the General Education Board a new organization was added — the Rockefeller Foundation, chartered under the laws of the State of New York, May 14, 1913, "to promote the well-being of mankind throughout the world." Within about a year of its incorporation, Mr. Rockefeller had placed in the hands of its trustees the sum of $100,000,000, since increased, by further gifts, to approximately $165,000,000, of which both interest and principal may be expended by the Foundation for its corporate purposes.

These purposes were exceedingly broad in scope. At first a few obligations were imposed by Mr. Rockefeller, but in 1919 he removed them all, so that the Trustees of the Foundation are now entirely free to expend both principal and interest as they wish. There have indeed been instances in which the Board has given its support to objects of its own choice rather than Mr. Rockefeller's. At first also the appropriations were somewhat miscellaneous in character, as on behalf of the Interstate Palisades Park on the Hudson and the National Bird Sanctuary in Louisiana. The advantage of such flexibility appeared especially in war-time, when, beginning with Belgian Relief, the Foundation appropriated in all $22,500,000 for the alleviation of human suffering due to the war in Europe.

In the course of a little more than ten years, however, the purposes of the Foundation have defined themselves with increasing clearness. They may now be said to lie especially in the wide fields of public health and medical education. The very names of the departments under which the work of the Foundation is organized testify to a recognition of the truth that "the war against disease is a world war." About each of these departments a tale of astonishing performance could be told. Here it is possible to speak only in the most general terms. The International Health Board, which in 1915 took over the work begun five years before by the Rockefeller Sanitary Commission for the Eradication of Hookworm, has made a world-wide extension of its successful effort to demonstrate the possibility of paving the way to vast economic and educational progress simply by conquering a disease which has rendered whole peoples backward. This work is now carried forward by local and national authorities in many regions at home and abroad. The China Medical Board is maintaining — to name but one of its many undertakings — the Peking Union Medical College, in which the effort, of undisputed value, at first a missionary effort to bring from the West to the East the best results of medical science, is most highly exemplified. The Division of Medical Education, besides forwarding by large appropriations the progress of higher medical studies in the United States, has carried the work to Canada, Brazil, and Europe, where especially it has promoted medical education in London, Edinburgh, Oxford, Cambridge, and Brussels. The International Health Board of the Foundation has helped to create or strengthen Schools of Public Health at Johns Hopkins, Harvard, the University of Toronto, and in London. The millions applied to these objects have been matched by other millions expended in all parts of the world. The Foundation maintains, besides, a Division of Studies, concerned with the development and observation of projects not included under any of the heads that have been named.

Nor is this list of Rockefeller benefactions yet complete. In memory of Mrs. John D. Rockefeller, who died in 1915 after a lifetime of intense sympathy with her husband's philanthropic enterprises, especially on behalf of the South and the Negro race, the Laura Spelman Rockefeller Memorial was established in 1918, with a fund of approximately $75,000,000 for forwarding humanitarian activities. In 1912 the Bureau of Social Hygiene, for "the study, amelioration, and prevention of those social conditions, crimes, and diseases which adversely affect the well-being of society," was established by Mr. John D. Rockefeller, Jr. And in 1922 the International Education Board was founded by this inheritor of the traditions and impulses of both his parents. If there is no new foundation to record for 1924, it was marked by the younger Mr. Rockefeller's personal gift of $1,000,000 to France for the restoration of the Cathedral of Rheims, and the palaces of Versailles and Fontainebleau; and early in 1926 came the announcement of his wish — now apparently frustrated — to dedicate a fund of $10,000,000 to the work of Egyptian archæology.

Is it through the fulfillment of the laws of compensation or of poetic justice that even as the activities of the Standard Oil Company have penetrated every corner of the earth, the Rockefeller benefactions have had for their physical boundaries the limits of the world itself?

IV

The cause with which this chapter has dealt is the cause of efficient giving on the magnificent scale which modern conditions have made possible. As champions of this cause, the Rockefellers, father and son, have been selected for the conspicuous example they have set. It is a new thing in the world to give more than half a billion dollars from a single fortune to objects in which its possessors believe. It is a new thing to put into the processes of giving the thought which has gone into the distribution of millions of income from the "benevolent trusts" which bear the Rockefeller name. These things are of a significance which matches their newness.

The financial and industrial trusts of the business world owe their success not only to a strong forma-

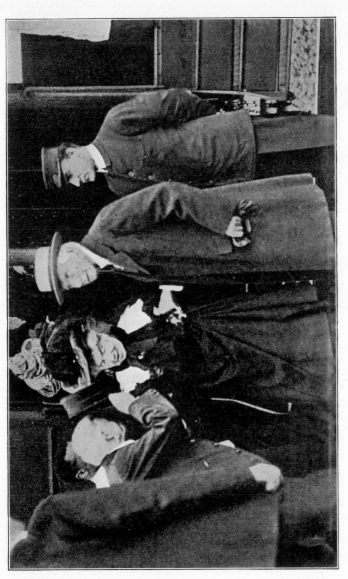

MR. AND MRS. JOHN D. ROCKEFELLER ARRIVING IN CLEVELAND ON THE
TWENTIETH CENTURY LIMITED

tive hand, but also to the joining together of powerful personal forces, working together for a common
end. This is paralleled in the various boards that
control the Rockefeller benefactions. At the headquarters of the Rockefeller Institute and at the
offices at 61 Broadway, New York City, where the
activities of the General Education Board and the
Rockefeller Foundation are centred, such executives
as Dr. George E. Vincent, Dr. Wallace Buttrick,
and Dr. Wickliffe Rose summon to their counsel
such men — to choose a few names almost at random from the past and present membership of all
the boards — as Dr. Simon Flexner and Mr. Abraham Flexner, Dr. Theobald Smith, Dr. William
Henry Welch, Dr. Charles W. Eliot, Andrew
Carnegie, Walter H. Page, Mr. John W. Davis,
President Angell of Yale, President Alderman of
Virginia, Mr. William Allen White, Mr. Vernon
Kellogg, Mr. Raymond B. Fosdick, and Mr. John
D. Rockefeller, Jr. To place in hands like theirs —
hands the most competent in education, science,
and affairs — the responsibility of administering
great agencies of public welfare is to ensure the
maximum of good and the minimum of that evil
which insists upon mixing itself into most human
undertakings.

This, indeed, is a danger squarely to be faced.

Is it safe to place in any hands — whether belonging, as in these instances, to self-perpetuating bodies, or even appointed by the State — such enormous power both economic and social as the Rockefeller boards must exercise? The boards are made up of fallible human beings, presumably quite conscious of their fallibility. However admirable their intentions, their performances, in the proof, may be open to grave question and criticism. As the lives of great endowments are measured, these enterprises are all in their infancy. Call them rather in their youth. Think of the annual crop of boys of great apparent promise. It seems as firmly fixed in the laws of nature that in a certain proportion of them the promise will fail as that the valedictorian will not always lead his class through life. In all these cases we cultivate our hopes, but, unless we are uncommonly stupid, we do not deny that there are also fears. It is for time to show which will prevail.

And as these are all new things, so are they distinctively American things. What governments and public subscriptions have done abroad — as in the establishment of the Pasteur Institute in Paris — individuals of great wealth have had the humanitarian and civic spirit to do in the United States. In a Bulletin of "American Foundations for Social Welfare," published in 1924 by the Russell Sage Foundation Library, seventy-five funds, of which forty-eight have been established by individuals or families for objects of human betterment, and, apparently with six exceptions, all since 1900, are catalogued. The Rockefeller and Carnegie funds lead the others in point of magnitude; but it is noticeable that the list, though enumerating besides the foundations fifty-one "Community Trusts," takes no account of what has been done in the same time for our colleges and universities.

One result of all this giving is that in many fields of higher knowledge there is now as much reason for European students to resort to the United States as for American students to go abroad. In the long recovery from the effects of the World War, a pressing economic need is likely for many years to come to retard the progress of advanced learning in Europe. Not for any pride of leadership, but to serve mankind throughout the world, America is now confronted, as never before, with the opportunity to add to the sum of human happiness by extending the boundaries of human knowledge, and by quickening the human spirit.

Such agencies as the Rockefeller endowments

are already contributing, directly and indirectly, to this end. Indirectly they are doing much more — in demonstrating to men and women of wealth that, when their own immediate needs and those of their families are met, there are the needs of mankind to be considered, and that in meeting them the deepest incentives and rewards for success are to be found. The Rockefellers have not worn their hearts on their sleeves, for all to read their inmost promptings. But there are many and valid tokens that what they have demonstrated is what they have lived — and it is of good omen that a democracy has been the scene of it all.

V

AMERICAN LABOR

SAMUEL GOMPERS LEADING

As the traveler in lands of the older world looks upon the ancient masonry of temples, pyramids, aqueducts, city walls, castles, and cathedrals, and turns his thought to former civilizations, he must see in the masses of stone piled upon stone the token of infinite human toil, the work of slaves, feudal servants, and armies. The emperor, bishop, or general, under whom these products of human energy, enduring through the centuries, were built, may live on as an historic name — and deservedly, for without his vision and directing power the work would never have been done. The workman is forgotten, inevitably forgotten, as merely one in a nameless multitude; yet, whatever his zeal for the cause in which even a monument of religion has reared its walls, he was still a human being, subject to hunger, thirst, and weariness, subject also to complete exploitation, usually — we may be sure — at hands none too sensitive. With nobody to speak for him, and incapable of speaking for himself, he could do merely as he was told, to the enrichment of architecture and the utter submergence of his own identity.

The individual worker in modern industry is still a member of an army, and even in this age of self-expression, without the power to imprint much, if any, of his personal identity upon his daily work. Since labor-saving power and machinery have in many instances supplanted the manual skill of individuals, this has become increasingly true. But the worker is no longer a silent pawn, to be played at the whim of his employer. In his town, his state, his country, the world at large, he is banded with other workers of his own and other trades, under leaders through whose voices his own, blending with those of thousands upon thousands, makes itself heard to effective purpose. The cathedrals of to-day could not be built at all were organized labor to say No.

In the single century now ending — and most notably in the second half of that century — there has come to pass a change in the condition of the working class as a whole which would have seemed unbelievable a hundred years ago. In this period of universal change economic and industrial forces never dreamed of when the century began have altered the whole relation between employer and employed. But for the constantly recurring appearance of powerful leaders for the forces of labor, the workers would have remained inarticulate, and the history of the "labor movement," with all its contribution to the general cause of human betterment, would still have to be made. It is, to be sure, still in the making — not through the fulfillment of any single tendency, but through the operation of many forces, highly complicated and diverse.

In the United States it is not too much to say that the history of the labor movement for the past forty years and more has been inseparable from the personal history of Samuel Gompers, the lifelong foe of socialism, of whom Mr. John Spargo, for many years, though not finally, an authoritative spokesman for that way of thinking, has recently written: "Mr. Gompers held his unique position by virtue of extraordinary gifts of intellect and character, amounting to something closely akin to genius. Taken all in all, he was incomparably the greatest leader that the trade-union movement of any country has yet produced." Still another writer, Mr. Benjamin Stolberg, has described Gompers as the Moses of American Labor, "through the forty years of its daily struggle for manna, its defense against inner rebellion and outer attack"; and he adds, "It is hard to tell Moses from Israel during those forty years in the desert." Because the leader and his people were so fused into a single force, they may best be regarded here as such, and so be treated. Let us then look upon them as one.

I

Samuel Gompers was an American by adoption, not by birth. Just opposite the home of his boyhood in London, where he was born January 27, 1850, there stood a silk factory, which the topographical biographer may identify, if he will and can, with the scene of Matthew Arnold's lines,

> And the pale weaver, through his windows seen
> In Spitalfields, look'd thrice dispirited.

It was a sordid, dispiriting neighborhood, and the young Gompers, surrounded by silk-weavers often out of work, had ample occasion for gaining an early knowledge of the hardships endured by the class into which he was born. His parents, Solomon and Sara (Rood) Gompers, were Dutch Jews who had moved from Amsterdam to London before their marriage. His grandfather Gompers, a man of no little personal dignity, was a dealer in antiques and, in pursuance of his calling, a considerable traveler. He and his family, including a son only ten months older than Sam, occupied the second floor of the house of which his father, mother, he, his four younger brothers, and a sister occupied the lower. After his parents moved from London to New York three more children were born to them. In outward circumstance their lives differed widely from those of earlier generations of the family, members of which — spelling their name Gomperz and otherwise — had distinguished themselves as rabbis, scholars, and generous men of wealth both in Holland and in Prussia.

To supplement the education imparted by a large and lively family circle, Sam Gompers was sent to a Jewish free school at six. At ten his earnings were needed for the family sustenance, and he went to work, still so eager for knowledge that he attended a night free school in which his mind received further training through study of the Talmud. But the formalities of the Jewish religion meant even less to him than to his imperfectly orthodox family. "By nature," he wrote many years later, "I am a nonconformist. I believe that restrictions dwarf personality and that largest usefulness comes through greatest personal freedom. Somehow I have never been able to separate an act of worship or service, as I prefer to call it, from some concrete human need."

Sam Gompers, so to call him again (he said that everybody who cared a cent about him called him

Sam), began his working life at ten in the shop
of a London shoemaker, but before long persuaded
his father to apprentice him instead to his own
trade of cigarmaking, for the reason that there
was a society among the cigarmakers which the
shoemakers lacked. Here was a characteristic beginning. It was also like him to seize every boyish
opportunity for cultivating a strong native liking,
that proved unfailing through life, for music and
the theatre. As the difficulty of supporting the
growing family of Solomon Gompers in London
grew constantly less manageable, the lure of
America began to exert itself. In the early sixties
our Civil War, stirring the ruling element of
England to little sympathy with the North, drew
the workers of that country to the side of the
Federal government as representing the cause of
industrial freedom. Indeed the trade unions of
England, through their stand against the use of
contraband cotton, even to their own hindrance,
bore a memorably important part in keeping the
British government out of the conflict. To these
larger considerations, however, the Gompers family
presumably gave little thought. None the less one
learns with interest that the youthful Sam Gompers
used to sing to his older fellow workers in the
cigar factory, with all the fervor of his being, the

popular songs of the day, "The Slave Ship" and "To the West, to the West, to the Land of the Free" — a ballad, as Andrew Carnegie afterwards told Gompers, which inspired the Scotch boy's father with the wish to emigrate to the United States. Yielding to the same desire, the Gompers family embarked on a sailing ship in London, June 10, 1863, and seven weeks and one day later were landed at Castle Garden in New York. Father and oldest son, thirteen years of age, both set to work immediately at their trade of cigarmaking. Within two years the boy had responded so completely to what is now called Americanization that a day of his fifteenth year stamped itself on his consciousness with the same sharpness of outline that it produced in multitudes of natives of his new country.

"I remember very vividly," writes Gompers in his autobiography, "the morning that brought the news of President Lincoln's death. It was Saturday. Like some cataclysm came the report that an assassin had struck down the great Emancipator. It seemed that some power for good had gone out of the world. A master mind had been taken at a time when most needed. I cried and cried all that day, and for days I could scarcely force myself to work."

If Gompers was already a complete American, it is clear from many tokens that in his earliest years he laid the foundations for the political and social credo which he pronounced in his middle life:

> In religion I am a workingman, and in every nerve, in every fibre, in every aspiration, I am on the side which will advance the interests of my fellow workingmen. . . . I represent my side, the side of the toiling, wage-earning masses, in every act and in my every utterance.

At the time when Gompers was beginning to work at his trade as a cigarmaker in New York, the American labor movement, as it is known to-day, was in a state hardly more than adolescent. It was born, to be sure, long before Gompers himself. Even in the eighteenth century workingmen in separate trades and towns had banded themselves together for the betterment of working conditions. The historians of labor place the actual beginning of the present movement in 1827, when the carpenters of Philadelphia struck for a ten-hour day and other organized workers brought their sympathetic support to the strike. By that time shoemakers, printers, carpenters, and other laborers had organized themselves in various places. The temper of the less towards the more fortunate in the American social order was signifi-

cantly expressed in a statement issued in 1830 by
the Workingmen's Republican Political Association of Penn Township in Philadelphia:

> There appear to exist two classes, the rich and the poor;
> the oppressor and the oppressed; those that live by their
> own labor and they that live by the labor of others; the
> aristocratic and the democratic; the despotic and republican,
> who are in direct opposition to one another in their objects
> and pursuits; the one aspiring to dignified station and offices
> of power, the other seeking for an equality of state and
> advantage —

with many further amplifications of the contrast
between the "haves" and the "have-nots."

There was indeed reason enough for a widespread sense of injustice. The labor of women
and children was shamefully exploited. Free public
schooling hardly existed in many flourishing communities until the workers made it a matter of
political insistence. Wages were so low that soon
after 1830 it was estimated that in the needle
trades a woman with children could not earn
more than $36.40 a year. At approximately the
same time a woman in Providence whose husband
lost his life in a fire was imprisoned for a debt of
sixty-eight cents to the owner of the burned building. In New York state an imprisonment for a
debt of twenty-five cents was recorded. The labor

strikes of the thirties and forties were frequently aimed at securing a ten- or even an eleven-hour working-day. The conditions of living appear to have been hardly so shocking as in England and Scotland in the earlier days of industrial development, but they were quite bad enough. And there was more incentive in America to change them for the better. Apart from the greater freedom of opportunity — of which the Free Homestead law of 1862, opening unoccupied land to many, was one expression — there was no universal Church Catechism teaching the young to do their duty in that state of life unto which it shall please God to call them, with the implied injunction to remain satisfied with that state. By the same token the English laboring class has doubtless been more conscious of itself as a class, and has therefore been carried further in the direction of political organization.

The Civil War, following a long period of industrial ups and downs, brought inevitably an industrial revival. Between 1863 and 1866 ten new national unions of workers at trades came into existence. By 1870 these national unions numbered more than thirty. For a period of six years, ending in 1872, there was an annual congress of the National Labor Union, in which it was endeavored, without ultimate success, to consolidate their interests. A short-lived Industrial Brotherhood, and an Order of Sovereigns of Industry, also a longer-lived Noble Order of Knights of Labor followed, but their sounding titles did not avail to render them permanent. The panic of 1873, the railroad strikes, and the "Molly Maguire" troubles of the same decade left the forces of labor, at the end of it, disorganized and discredited, but ready for the revival destined for the early eighties.

By this time Gompers had passed through the formative experiences which made him what he was, both as a man and as a labor leader. The very nature of the trade on which he had entered — that of cigarmaking — had an important bearing on his development. In frequent early conflict with employers who would make it a tenement rather than a factory industry, he made his own daily contribution to it as a factory worker, and the shop itself became a strong educative influence. As the workers sat at their separate benches, using their fingers to the height of their skill, there was every occasion for cultivating not only a sense of comradeship and brotherhood but also a community of thought on matters of real concern to the shopmates. Gompers himself has suggested these conditions:

I loved the freedom of that work, for I had earned the mind-freedom that accompanied skill as a craftsman. I was eager to learn from discussion or reading or to pour out my feeling in song. Often we chose someone to read to us who was a particularly good reader, and in payment the rest of us gave him sufficient of our cigars so he was not the loser. The reading was always followed by discussion, so we learned to know each other pretty thoroughly. We learned who could take a joke in good spirit, who could marshal his thoughts in an orderly way, who could distinguish clever sophistry from sound reasoning. The fellowship that grew between congenial shopmates was something that lasted a lifetime.

At another point in his autobiography he writes:

Anyone who does not know the cigarmaking trade will find it difficult to appreciate the educational value of the little forum existing in each shop. It gave education in such a way as to develop personality, for in no other place were we so wholly natural. The nature of our work developed a camaraderie of the shop such as few workers enjoy. It was a world in itself — a cosmopolitan world. Shopmates came from everywhere. When they told us of strange lands and peoples we listened eagerly. No one ever questioned another as to his past life, for many were revolutionists who sought new opportunity and safety by leaving the past blank.

If these were not "educational advantages," as a youth like Sam Gompers might employ them,

the term is hard to define. He extended them
liberally by a thoughtful daily reading of the
New York Sun, under the stimulating editorship of
Charles A. Dana, and by attending devotedly
through many years the classes and lectures provided by the Cooper Union for the people of the
East Side. "Nothing humanly possible," he wrote
long afterwards, "ever kept me from attending
those Saturday night lectures. I was fairly quivering in my intense desire to know. Mental hunger
is just as painful as physical hunger." Abounding
alike in physical and mental vigor, Gompers early
and late fed his mind as plentifully as he gratified
his hearty appetite for food and drink.

Of the many personal influences that touched
Gompers through these formative years there was
none more potent than that of his friend Ferdinand
Laurrell, a cigarmaker of Swedish birth and cosmopolitan experience, partly in Germany. Under
his guidance Gompers taught himself German in
order to read first the Communist Manifesto and
afterwards the writings of Karl Marx and others.
Laurrell believed strongly in the trade-union principle applied to existing industrial conditions and
disbelieved, as strongly, in socialism. He saw the
promise of leadership in Gompers, and gave him
a bit of advice remembered with lasting gratitude:

"Never permit sentiment to lead you, but let intellect dominate action." Gompers was firmly persuaded that this anti-utopian counsel saved him from many mistakes. As the years went on his antipathy to all radicalism increased. In the early days of his labor leadership he was enough of a radical to say of the movement, in its political aspects, "While keeping in view a lofty ideal, we must advance towards it through practical steps, taken with intelligent regard for pressing needs. I believe with the most advanced thinkers as to ultimate ends, including abolition of the wage system." Towards the end of his life, in recording a disagreement with a socialist, he declared, "Socialists the world over are of the same mental calibre; there is only one way to deal with them — don't argue, just tell them." The gentle and able Laurrell — as Gompers characterized him — could hardly have realized how far his pupil would go.

That Gompers was essentially a realist the record of his domestic life appears to show as clearly as that of his broader social relations. An avowed believer in the institution of the family, he translated his belief early and completely into practice. The story of his marriage to the mother of his many children is singularly lacking in romance.

As he tells it himself, a friend said to him one day, when he was sixteen years old, "Sam, I've got to go away for the summer. Will you look after my girl for me?" The girl, Sophia Julian, six months younger than himself, was also a native of London, and worked in the same shop with him. Sam, true to the promise he had made to his friend, began to "look after" her. The friend had then done well to return and look after him, for on the day he was seventeen, January 27, 1867, the boy and girl, with another young couple with whom they had been sharing many simple pleasures, fell to discussing how the birthday might best be celebrated.

Someone [writes Gompers] suggested that we get married. Sophie did not show any disposition to oppose. It was too late to carry out the plan that night, so we determined on the following day. On January 28, without consultation or announcement of plans, we simply went to the justice of the peace at the city hall of Brooklyn and we were married. Jack and Mary stood up for us as witnesses and we stood up for them, and so both couples were married.

All this is related as naïvely as he goes on a little later in the autobiography to describe his married life:

Soon afterward we set up our own nest — only two rooms, but our own. Before I was eighteen I had a father's responsibility for a son and regularly thereafter a newcomer found its way into that nest every two years. We had n't much, but we were bound together by a common fate. I could not understand irresponsibility of word or act.

The sense of responsibility could not have sprung full-grown into being. Quite unabashed, Gompers tells of his wife handing him one day twenty-five dollars that she had saved with much difficulty — lack of employment in New York had driven them for a time to Hackensack — and asking him to spend it, through his mother, on the material for two dresses for herself. On the way to his mother's house he made the mistake of visiting his wife's father, in whose shop the musical instruments for sale tempted him beyond his powers of resistance. The father-in-law, loath at first to see his daughter's savings spent on a violin for the young man instead of on dresses for herself, yielded also to temptation, and sent the defaulter away, fiddle under arm, to make such peace as he could with his wife in her disappointment — and the neighbors in their rage at the horrible sounds his untutored fingers drew from the instrument.

His autobiography has been censured for the author's failure to reveal any depths of feeling in his family relationships. Possibly they were not of the deepest. Yet when Gompers writes, apropos

of the death of a beloved daughter, the tidings
of which reached him in Italy in 1918, "I cannot
describe the experience I passed through — I would
not if I could," there is no suggestion of insensi-
tiveness; nor is it to be found in the story of his
dealings with the doctor who, on learning that
Gompers was penniless, refused to superintend the
birth of a son afterwards dubbed the "strike
baby," born at a moment of unemployment when
there was no money in the house. "You will come
with me now," said Gompers to the reluctant
doctor, taking his collar in hand, "or you will
never make another move." He came, and was
duly paid for his visit. Here he shows his feeling
clearly enough; and again, in an instance affecting
his personal integrity. It was charged, when a
treasurer of Cigarmakers' Local No. 144 misap-
propriated the funds in his keeping, that Gompers,
then president of the Local, had profited from the
dishonesty. "Their charge," says the autobiography, "produced such an effect upon me that in
walking away from there to my home, for the
first and only time of my life I fainted — fainted in
the streets and was carried to my home, where I
was in a delirious condition for more than twenty-
four hours."

In "Mother Gompers" he had a sturdy ally.

Once when he was out of work and blacklisted, another cigarmaker called on Mrs. Gompers and offered her thirty dollars a week for three months if she would induce her husband to leave the union and return to work. When Gompers came home and heard what had happened, "I turned to my wife," he writes, "and said, 'Well, what did you tell him?' My wife, indignant at the question, answered, 'What do you suppose I said to him, with one child dying and another coming? Of course I took the money.' Stunned by the blow, I fell in a chair. My wife, all tenderness and sympathy, seeing I did n't understand, exclaimed: 'Good God, Sam, how could you ask such a question? Don't you know I resented the insult?'"

Gompers wrote of himself, "I am a sport in the general acceptance of the term. I am a man's man with a few of a man's virtues." Whatever light this may throw upon his relations with family, friends, and associates, it is a fact that he had that capacity for exciting and maintaining a strong sense of devotion which belongs to a dominant personality concentrated on a single purpose. This purpose, for him, was the betterment of the conditions of existence for wage-earners — not by any change in the structure of industrial society, but through the influence and pressure of trade-unions towards securing from employers better wages, shorter hours, increase of opportunity for developing the individual into a more civilized human being. If his watchword of "More, more, more, and now" was primarily opportunist, his other saying, "I want the stars in heaven for the toilers," represented the ultimate goal of his endeavor.

Certain influences which started him towards this goal have already been suggested. Among the others, contributing largely to the development of his personality, was the social quality in him which made him early and persistently a "joiner." Besides the Cigarmakers' Local there were in his younger days the Ancient Order of Foresters and the Independent Order of Odd Fellows and many less formal associations, in most of which he assumed the responsibilities not only of membership but of office-holding. Thus he acquired much knowledge of parliamentary technique and much experience in speaking on his feet. In his own trade-union he gained at the same time a first-hand familiarity with the warfare of strikes, the weapons of which are famous for cutting both ways. He tasted the bitterness of frequent defeats, the sweetness of occasional victories. Through outward circumstance in many forms he was receiving, especially through the decade of his twenties, an exceptionally thorough preparation for the task that lay before him.

II

In 1881 a number of representatives of separate trade-unions throughout the country met and formed the Federation of Organized Trades and Labor Unions of the United States and Canada. At the third convention of this body, in 1883, Samuel Gompers was elected chairman of its legislative committee and first vice-president of the Federation, of which he became president when the man elected resigned. In 1886 this organization became the American Federation of Labor, and Gompers immediately became its president, holding the post continuously — except for the year 1894-95, when a socialist opposition joined with a body of miners to compass his defeat — for the nearly forty remaining years of his life.

It is often said that he imposed upon the Federation the rigid and generally conservative views which he held at the beginning of this period. It is no less to be said that a great body, representing at first some 150,000 workers and finally about 3,000,000, could not have been held to any fixed programme that was contrary to the wishes of the majority. In other words, a leader cannot remain indefinitely in the lead unless most of his followers are with him. Mere force of personality will accomplish wonders for a short time, but it is incredible that for forty years Gompers could have maintained his government of the Federation without the full consent and agreement of the mass of the governed. If Gompers was the American Federation of Labor, the Federation was in the main also Gompers.

Labor unions are divided into a variety of types. As against the industrial union, joining all the workers in a single industry regardless of their several crafts, Gompers was a firm believer in the trade union, made up of the workers in a single craft, and in a Federation bringing these workers together on the basis of their individual forms of labor.

True trade-unionists [he declared, in terms which he never modified,] are those wage-workers, members in good standing of the union of the trade or calling at which they are employed, who realize as a fundamental principle the necessity of unity of all their fellows employed at the same trade or calling; who recognize the vital, logical extension, growth, and development of all unions of all trades and callings; and who strive for the unity, federation, coöperation, fraternity, and solidarity of all organized wage-earners; who can and do subordinate self for the common good and always strive for the common uplift; who decline to limit the sphere of their activity by any dogma, doctrine, or ism. Finally, those organized wage-workers are true trade-unionists who fearlessly and insistently maintain that the trade unions are paramount to any other form of organization or movement of labor in the world.

Here is a positive statement of a positive theory. When the American Federation of Labor entered the field, the Knights of Labor, an organization of considerable magnitude and power, was undertaking, as Gompers saw it, "to make one organization of all classes of labor." He expressed well his objection to this scheme of organization when he said, "It would be just as impractical for purposes of achieving anything in the interest of the working people as it would be if applied to the different divisions of men in an army corps, perhaps cavalrymen, artillerymen, infantrymen, foot and horse soldiers, all being mixed up in a great potpourri. Chaos and confusion would reign if an order were given it to advance."

The Knights of Labor fell also into the classification of the "uplift union," with radical and utopian aims. The American Federation of Labor is, on the contrary, a "business union," based upon taking things as they are and, by pursuing policies which have often seemed equally radical to extreme conservatives and conservative to extreme radicals, to press at one point after another for the gradual improvement of conditions. For a few years the Knights, led by Terence V. Powderly, and the Federation, led by Gompers, were at swords' points. Now for many years it has been necessary to say, in significant condensation of what occurred, the Knights *were*, the Federation *is*.

To suggest the starting-point from which the Federation set out on its pilgrimage it is worth while to enumerate seven of the fourteen points of proposed legislation recommended by the Committee on Platform at the convention which formed the Federation of Trades and Labor Unions in 1881. These were: compulsory education laws, prohibition of labor of children under fourteen years, sanitary and safety provisions for factories, national eight-hour law, prohibition of contract convict labor, protection of American industry against cheap foreign labor, and laws prohibiting importation of foreign workers under contract. There was also from the first a strict determination to abstain, as an organization, from party politics. "We must be partisan for a principle," said Gompers, "and not for a party"; and in the constitution of the Federation itself it is written that "party politics, whether they be Democratic,

Republican, Socialistic, Populistic, Prohibition, or any other, shall have no place in the conventions of the American Federation of Labor." In practice the general plan of the regular trade unionist, politically, has been to reward the friends and punish the enemies of his cause. This has not been inconsistent with the constant, organized exertion of pressure on State Legislatures and Congress for the enactment of laws favorable to labor. The adoption of the national Eight-Hour Law of 1912, the creation of a Department of Labor in 1913, and the passage of the Clayton Anti-Trust Law in 1914 were conspicuous fruits of this effort. The principles of the "trade agreement" by "collective bargaining," of coöperation with the National Civic Federation, representing the employer class, and of the organization of women's trade-unions, have taken their place with many other objects of endeavor in the general programme. The total record of arrivals at clearly defined objectives between 1881 and the present time is substantial to a degree that could hardly have been contemplated at the beginning.

All this called for strong qualities of personal leadership, organization, and administration. Gompers possessed these qualities in abundance. A lover of life and men, of broad sympathies with

SAMUEL GOMPERS
FROM "AN AUTOBIOGRAPHY OF SEVENTY YEARS OF
LIFE AND LABOR"

the under dogs of human society, of tireless vitality, a fighter ready both to give and to take hard
blows, he was made to lead just such a cause as
that to which he gave himself. At the beginning
of his leadership his own resources and those of
the Federation were of the slenderest. Such as they
were, he developed and organized them all. As
the Federation grew in strength, wealth, and influence, with a building of its own in Washington,
with innumerable contacts with the labor movement on one side and the government on the
other, the demands upon his powers grew steadily
greater, and with this growth his capacity to deal
with large issues, if not his conception of their
nature, kept pace.

One unquestioned source of his strength was
his personal integrity. At various times in his
career opportunities to better himself financially
presented themselves and were put aside, so that
his freedom as a spokesman for labor remained
unfettered. To the temptations to which the office-
holders of the movement are often exposed — the
softening influences of prosperity, the allurements
of politics and capital, the mahogany-table attitude
of mind — he held himself immune. He liked
alcoholic drink, — and hated prohibition when it
came, as he hated all compulsion, — but escaped

habits of intemperance which would have impaired his usefulness. In his powerful carrying voice and cocksure mind, untroubled by subtleties, his hail-fellow-well-met manner of dealing with men of every kind, he possessed invaluable attributes for a labor leader. His personal appearance, suggesting in many of his pictures a militant frog, has been so clearly recalled by Mr. Benjamin Stolberg in an article published in the *Atlantic Monthly* soon after the labor-leader's death that the portrait in words may well be reproduced:

Gompers had the physical spell of the personal leader. When seated, the powerful, long-armed torso and the enormous head seemed to belong to a six-footer. But when he arose, his hefty, absurd little legs kept him from soaring above five feet four and gave a touch of anthropoid strength to his chronic restlessness. The head was magnificent. It looked like an animated boulder, on which the weathers of a rich and dangerous life had carved large and rugged yet tremulously sensitive features. The granite complexion, the mossy tufts of graying hair, the Oriental cast of countenance — its whole noble freakishness fascinated. His face was perpetually acute, forever approving or disapproving with the entire gamut of strong emotion. When he felt very intensely his pellucid gray eyes, perched wide apart behind bits of window-glass, gave the impression of inflaming his face. The mouth was a wide slit, with the corners quivering down the hard and well-rounded jaw. The voice had the rare and exquisite gift of communicating any emotion he felt. All his vital expressions rose and fell together as though controlled by some inner mechanism. One moment the mobile mask would be cunningly furtive and quizzical, then intimately and wistfully kind; then again it would glow with a self-righteous passion that in retrospect seemed grotesque. It was a congenitally histrionic face, and its outlay in spiritual energy bespoke enormous vitality.

A much more extended portrait of Gompers is to be found in his two-volume autobiography, *Seventy Years of Life and Labor*, delivered to his publishers at the end of 1923, but not published until the spring of 1925, several months after his death. It is in effect a protracted speech of self-explanation and justification. It chronicles the labor movement of his time and is packed with incident and anecdote that illuminate his contemporaries and, still more, Gompers himself. Out of its pages peers forth the man whose acquaintance we have been making — perhaps a little idealized and egotized in the reflections from his own mirror, perhaps over-engrossed in a sort of triumphal progress through life, but essentially the man he was. At times the reader seems to be listening to one side of a debate, in which it is easy from the very nature of much that is said to divine what the other side is saying. In all that Gompers has to say about the errors of socialists, radicals, and "intellectuals" in general, — and let us not forget that his final recipe for dealing with socialists was "don't argue, just tell them," — in his expressions of opinion regarding such matters as court injunctions, compulsory arbitration, sundry famous strikes, and the leading figures helpful and malign, in the long conflict between capital and labor, his narrative leaves no doubt where Gompers — and his opponents — stood.

There are important points which, perhaps too discreetly, he leaves alone. There is no mention, for example, of the episode of President Roosevelt's reinstatement of an assistant foreman of the Government Printing Office, after losing his place because of his expulsion from a labor union — an incident that was closed by Roosevelt's vigorous reply to the protest of Gompers on behalf of the American Federation of Labor: "In the employment and dismissal of men in the government service I can no more recognize the fact that a man does or does not belong to a union than I can recognize the fact that he is a Protestant or a Catholic, a Jew or a Gentile, as being for or against him." Nothing is said about the intervention of Gompers in favor of the striking policemen of Boston and Governor Calvin Coolidge's reply, fraught with moment in his approach to the Presidency: "There is no right to strike against the public safety by anybody, anywhere, any time." One must look elsewhere, moreover, for any account of the debate between Gompers and Governor Allen of Kansas on the Industrial Relations Court of the state, when Gompers was forced to evade his antagonist's question about the rights of the public in a strike affecting the production and distribution of the necessaries of life, and subsequently issued the unsatisfying rejoinder: "The public has no rights which are superior to the toiler's right to live and to his right to defend himself against oppression."

After all, the autobiographers like Pepys and Cellini, who are not steadily bent upon putting their best foot forward, are few, and it is no wonder that Gompers, of necessity a lifelong special pleader, was not of their number.

III

When Gompers found himself in the winter and spring of 1919 established in offices at the Hotel Crillon in Paris as the presiding officer of the Commission on International Labor Legislation, appointed to present the views of organized labor throughout the world to the makers of the Treaty of Versailles, he may be said to have reached the climax of his career. To this post of world-importance he came by the natural steps of the influence he wielded as a labor leader before the war and of the position he took immediately upon its outbreak. Before 1914 he was what he called a doctrinaire pacifist, and frequently lifted his voice on behalf of movements towards organized peace on earth. In that very year he had placed in the hands of the Carnegie Peace Foundation a collection of his addresses on international peace for publication. "Jarred out of the complacency of pacifism" by the outbreak of the war in Europe, he instantly withdrew the manuscript, and from that time forth gave himself heart and soul to fighting the forces in which he saw "German aggrandizement under the domination of autocracy, militarism, and Kaiserism."

The course he was called upon to steer was anything but simple. The agency of strikes was capable of employment to work advantage either to labor or to Germany, and the distinction was not always apparent. Before the United States entered the war Gompers exerted his powerful influence towards stabilizing the labor situation in general. When American participation in the conflict became imminent, he accepted President

Wilson's appointment to the Advisory Commission of the Council of National Defense as the representative of labor. Mr. Grosvenor B. Clarkson, secretary of the Commission at the time, tells in his book, *Industrial America in the World War*, how Gompers read with great emotion one day at a meeting of the Commission his call to American labor to give its services "in every field of activity to defend, safeguard, and preserve the Republic of the United States of America against its enemies." And Mr. Clarkson declares, "There can be no doubt that in this contingency the veteran labor leader was first an American and a special pleader for labor afterwards."

Such indeed was his general course through the war. To the winning of it the steady contribution of the workers in the factories was essential, and great credit belongs to Gompers for having kept it steady. A letter from a Massachusetts manufacturer who during the war joined with a labor leader in counsel with the head of the Massachusetts Committee of Public Safety and Federal Food Administrator, the late Henry B. Endicott, lies before me. It testifies to the great value of the help that Endicott, even in New England, received from Gompers. Again and again when strikes were imminent, and labor seemed unwilling to submit the point in dispute to arbitration, the intervention of Gompers, through a letter or telegram from Washington, would save the day for uninterrupted production. His opponents in the ranks of labor blamed him for having failed to turn the opportunity which the time presented to greater immediate and subsequent account for the workers. It satisfied him on the whole to keep unlowered the standards of demand and recognition for which he had fought all his life. It was a further satisfaction to bear a leading part in contributing to the Treaty of Versailles a definition of the principles affecting the status of labor, and extending to the world at large some of the principles on which the American Federation of Labor was erected. It was not indeed that he got all he hoped for, but all that the conflicting circumstances would permit.

In a world of contrasts there are few more striking than those to be found in the life of Samuel Gompers. The head of the Commission on International Labor Legislation, in his office at the Crillon, must sometimes have pinched himself to make sure that he and the Dutch-English-Hebrew emigrant boy, the obscure little cigar-maker who had landed at Castle Garden more than fifty years before, were one and the same

person. Yet in his nearer approach to this post
of high responsibility he had stood before kings, —
in England, Belgium, and Italy, — had met on
equal terms with admirals and generals of the
allied forces, had visited the front, — where he
could not resist the impulse to make a labor
speech to a group of Canadian soldiers, — and
had fought the battles of his own labor beliefs
with British and Continental holders of opposing
views. These were some of the culminating pieces
of preparation for his work in Paris. There and
elsewhere he was in sympathy with most of the
views and policies of President Wilson, who had
appeared in person at the American Federation
of Labor convention of 1917, and had said of
Gompers, "I want to express my admiration of
his patriotic courage, his large vision, and his
statesman-like sense of what has to be done." His
work through the war and at Paris quite justified
the President's words.

Like many believers in the League of Nations,
through which it was assumed that the United
States would participate in the labor programme of
the Treaty, Gompers suffered grievous disappoint-
ments after the war. Before the Treaty was rejected by the United States Senate he attended an
international labor conference at Amsterdam in

August 1919, and, unwilling to countenance any substitution of revolutionary principle for the more conservative position of the American Federation of Labor, was largely responsible for the withdrawal of that body from the International Federation — a proceeding which incurred the deep censure of "the Left" in labor councils. Then the steel strike of 1919, which Gompers would have liked to avert, was lost. Other strikes, such as those of the bituminous coal miners and the "outlaw" railway men, suffered the same fate. Though the workers in general had shown themselves unready to follow the more radical leaders of the I. W. W., — rejoicing in such songs as "Hallelujah, I am a bum," — the unions managed to lose something of public confidence and approval in the years immediately succeeding the war. But Gompers showed no loss of zest in the work of his lifetime. "Frequently," he wrote of his final years, "there comes over me a feeling like liquid fire — it just courses through my veins — a yearning to work."

Failing health and the death of his wife in 1920 could not quench him. "My work was not yet finished," says his autobiography, "and it was not in my nature to live alone. Love and life were to me inseparable, so I found another helpmate and began life anew at seventy-one." Gertrude Annesley Gleaves, whom he had met long before in the house of her father at Trenton, New Jersey, became his second wife two years after the death of his first, who had shared his fortunes for fifty-three years. "Her world," he wrote of the younger woman so soon to become his widow, "had been that of art and music and we enjoyed beautiful things together, as the time had come when I could permit myself more of the things for which I had longed for years."

It was completely characteristic of Gompers to die "with his boots on." Through the spring and summer of 1924 he was seriously ill. From his sick-room he did what he could to advance the candidacy of Senator LaFollette for the presidency. In the autumn, badly broken in health, he faced the fatigues of an American Federation of Labor convention at El Paso, Texas, and of meeting delegates from the Mexican Federation convention at Juarez, in session across the border. General Calles was about to be inaugurated President of Mexico, and as a friend both of the man and of his country, Gompers decided to take part in the ceremonies and in an immediately ensuing Congress of the Pan-American Federation of Labor. It was manifest that the effort might be his last, but he could not be deterred from making it, cost what it might. He reached Mexico City November 30, 1924, and for a week met the exhausting demands upon the strength of one recognized as a powerful friend of Mexican and international labor. On Wednesday, December 8, the state of his heart was so alarming that the best hope for his recovery seemed to lie in his removal to Washington, and the long journey began. His ebbing strength cut it short at San Antonio, where he died December 13, 1924.

Of the honors accorded to the body of Gompers on the way to its Jewish and Masonic burial at Sleepy Hollow on the Hudson, the opening of the President's room in the Washington railway station to receive it was typical. In the circles of labor as in the community at large it was felt that a great leader of men had quitted the national scene, and, without putting it into the words of Carlyle, there were doubtless many who shared his thought: "This that they call the organization of labor is the universal vital problem of the world."

In what has been written here the mere fringe of an immense subject has been touched. The career of Gompers is by itself a large field of human study. The progress of labor during the forty years of his leadership is a vastly larger topic. An adequate treatment of it would include a full consideration of tendencies constantly opposed by Gompers and a long procession of men with whom he was in conflict. Before his death one of these opponents, Mr. W. Z. Foster, described him as "the arch-reactionary, the idol of all the holdbacks in the labor movement," declaring besides that, "considered as labor organizer, he is a first-class failure." In the view of this antagonist of later years — and his opinion of Gompers is by no means unique — the revolutionists in the labor movement should join the American Federation of Labor and work from within. "Keep the militants in the organized masses," he urges, "at all costs." Gompers himself took satisfaction in the thought that he and his policies were objectionable equally, and often on the same grounds, to the radicals of labor and to the conservatives of capital. Certain it is that he kept the middle of the road — the classic path of safety.

On the foundations he laid, what structure will now rise? The old fight, between those who would destroy industrial society before rebuilding it entire and those who would improve it by orderly repairs, will go on. Happily there is unanimity on one point in all the opposing camps —

that enlightenment of the mind will open the surest road to the better state of things which, in different forms, all are seeking. The ideals animating trade-unionism have been excellently defined as "brotherhood, education, a standard of living, and industrial freedom." To these ends Gompers, with human fallibilities and limitations, devoted a life of remarkable energy, honesty, and singleness of aim. Those who follow him will do well — whatever changes of policy and method the needs of the future may demand — to emulate him in the exercise of these qualities.

VI

WOMAN SUFFRAGE AND ITS NAPOLEON

SUSAN B. ANTHONY

WRITERS about Woman with a capital W are fond of alluding to an amazing definition of their subject in the first edition of a famous encyclopædia. The thing, when I encountered it, seemed too good to be true, but, to place the matter beyond question, I turned to the third and last volume of the *Encyclopædia Britannica* as it was first printed in Edinburgh in 1771. There indeed stands this immortal line: "WOMAN, the female of man. See HOMO." To see it through, I saw "HOMO." Fifteen lines were devoted to him, with not a word about Woman. I learned, however, that Linnæus ranks man under the order of primates, and divides him into two species, *homo sapiens* and *homo troglodytes*. Homo sapiens is subdivided into five varieties, the American, the European, the Asiatic, the African, and what he calls "the monstrous." Under this heading the eighteenth-century encyclopædists would probably have ranked the newest New Woman had she been available for classification in 1771. Long before that, Saint Chrysostom, framing a list of neatly worded definitions of woman in general, gave one of them as "a desirable calamity" — not so far from "the monstrous" of Linnæus. In the latest edition of the *Britannica*, Woman, as a separate subject, is treated with the greatest seriousness in a number of pages, ending with a bibliography for further reading calculated to occupy an inquiring mind for months.

Such is the change that has come in a century and a half. In fact it may be said to have come in half that period, for in spite of such tokens of the impending as the publication, in 1790, of *A Vindication of the Rights of Women*, by Mary Wollestonecraft, — whose daughter, Mary Godwin, became the wife of Shelley, — it was not until about 1850 that the "Woman Movement" assumed serious proportions. With its progress in America no single figure was more conspicuously, or more effectively, identified than Susan B. Anthony.

Nor was there in the whole nineteenth-century company of American "come-outers" and reformers a more typical figure than Miss Anthony.

ECCENTRIC

BIOGRAPHY;

OR,

MEMOIRS OF REMARKABLE

FEMALE CHARACTERS

ANCIENT AND *MODERN.*

INCLUDING,

ACTRESSES	GIPSIES
ADVENTURERS	DWARFS
AUTHORESSES	SWINDLERS AND
FORTUNETELLERS	VAGRANTS.

ALSO MANY OTHERS
WHO HAVE DISTINGUISHED THEMSELVES BY THEIR
CHASTITY, DISSIPATION, INTREPIDITY, LEARN-
ING, ABSTINENCE, CREDULITY,

&c. &c.

ALPHABETICALLY ARRANGED,
FORMING A PLEASING MIRROR OF REFLECTION TO THE

FEMALE MIND.

𝔚𝔬𝔯𝔠𝔢𝔰𝔱𝔢𝔯 :
PRINTED BY ISAIAH THOMAS, JUN :
For B. *&* J. HOMANS·
SOLD BY THEM AND THOMAS & WHIPPLE, NEWBURYPORT
*April—*1804. •

A FEMINIST TITLE-PAGE, 1804
AN ADVANCE ON THE FIRST BRITANNICA

To say that your true reformer is so in love with his — or her — work that all its hardships, physical, mental, and social, are really to be counted among its satisfactions and rewards, is not at all to disparage the reformer. In the very nature of the case, the reformer is a "disturbing element," a very pestilence to all the comfortable folk who are content to let well enough alone. There must have been something quite unlovely in many representatives of the contemporary type to which Miss Anthony belonged. Barrett Wendell found, among the men, Whittier "the least irritating of the reformers." Henry James was manifestly thinking of some woman reformer known to his American youth when he described a character in *The Bostonians* in these terms:

Mrs. Farrinder, at almost any time, had the air of being introduced by a few remarks. She talked with great slowness and distinctness, and evidently a high sense of responsibility; she pronounced every syllable of every word and insisted on being explicit. If, in conversation with her, you attempted to take anything for granted, or to jump two or three steps at a time, she paused, looking at you with a cold patience, as if she knew that trick, and then went on at her own measured pace. She lectured on temperance and the rights of women; the ends she labored for were to give the ballot to every woman in the country and to take the flowing bowl from every man.

This is precisely what Miss Anthony did, but if in her younger days she was ever such a woman as Mrs. Farrinder the testimony of her friends leaves no reason to believe that she continued so to the end, or anywhere near it. She was none the less a typical reformer — subjected to incredible fatigues and discouragements, ridiculed and abused, yet unshaken in her devotion to the cause to which she had consecrated her heart, brain, and bodily strength, and apparently no more abased through failures than exalted through triumphs, indeed just as truly the "happy warrior" as her friend Frances Willard. Her cause and her character are equally worthy of study — the one as a cause to the slow winning of which her pioneering and long-sustained effort made a vast contribution, the other as a character remarkable in itself and highly typical of the nineteenth-century "come-outer."

I

Susan B. Anthony was nearly thirty years old when she entered the field of active work as a reformer. It is easy to place her chronologically in relation to the mid-year of the nineteenth century, for in 1850 she reached the age of thirty. Her actual entrance to the reform field came through the avenues of temperance and antislavery, in each of which her active interest began shortly before 1850. In 1852 she attended her first Woman's Rights convention, and from that time until her death in 1906, fifty-four years later, she poured into the cause of woman suffrage a flood of energy, ability, and character from which an enormous generation of power proceeded.

It would be absurd to blame anybody for a failure seventy-five years ago to foresee the extent to which the political, social, and economic disabilities resting upon women entirely because of their sex were destined to removal long before they won the right to vote. It is easy, on the other hand, to understand how women — and men — endowed with a strong sense of justice must have resented these disabilities. Against the approach of women many doors of education were closed, even locked. The gainful occupations open to them were few, and restricted in character. What they earned, if they happened to be married, belonged to their husbands, as did the control of such property as they might possess. The destinies of children were in the hands of fathers rather than mothers, in that a father, at death, could name the guardian of a child without reference to the mother's wishes. This, in general, was the condition based upon the workings of the English common law, many implications of which are found in the fact that a husband was forbidden to chastise his wife with a stick bigger than his own thumb. The condition began to be mended in America when the New York Assembly in 1848, after twelve years of discussion, passed a law enlarging the property rights of married women. In the same year, 1848, the first Woman's Rights Convention was held at Seneca Falls, New York, and was soon followed by another at Rochester.

A famous Declaration of Sentiments, adopted at the Seneca Falls Convention, is worth recalling for its significance as a starting-point in the organized agitation for woman suffrage. After the Convention had been called by four women, of whom Lucretia Mott and Elizabeth Cady Stanton bore the two names destined to widest familiarity, they found themselves confronted with the necessity of preparing a statement which should place their cause before the assemblage and the outside public in the strongest possible terms. In the process of casting about for the form it should take, one of them read aloud the Declaration of Independence, and the quartette decided at once to base their own declaration upon this historic document. It was an audacious thing to do, and could hardly have been better calculated to provoke antagonism and ridicule.

In the Preamble several small but significant changes were called for. The self-evident truth that "all men are created equal" was replaced by another: that "all men and women are created equal." For the sentence, "The history of the present King of Great Britain is a history of repeated injuries and usurpations, all having in direct object the establishment of an absolute tyranny over these States," the new Declaration substituted, "The history of mankind is a history of repeated injuries and usurpations on the part of man toward woman, having in direct object the establishment of an absolute tyranny over her." Since the original document contained a list of eighteen grievances, it was thought necessary to provide an equal number, and, apparently with some difficulty, — and some assistance from men who joined in the search for them, — the eighteen were found. In the Declaration of Independence it will be remembered that all the grievances in the list begin with the words, "He has" — the personal pronoun referring to King George. In the Declaration of Sentiments the same "He has" makes its eighteen appearances, but "He" refers to Man. The first grievance, sounding clearly the

war cry of the long fight that lay ahead, was:
"He has never permitted her to exercise her in-
alienable right to the elective franchise." The
eighteenth — a climax of generalization following
the specific charges of masculine tyranny — was
thus defined: "He has endeavored, in every way
that he could, to destroy her confidence in her
own powers, to lessen her self-respect, and to make
her willing to lead a dependent and abject life."

The document bristled with challenge to the
existing social order. If it meant anything, it
"meant business"; and the sixty-eight women
and thirty-two men who signed it — an even
hundred in all — must have realized to what an
enterprise they were committing themselves. On
this point the paragraph with which the declaration ended was unequivocal:

In entering upon the great work before us, we anticipate
no small amount of misconception, misrepresentation, and
ridicule; but we shall use every instrumentality within our
power to effect our object. We shall employ agents, circulate tracts, petition the State and National legislatures, and
endeavor to enlist the pulpit and press in our behalf. We
hope this Convention will be followed by a series of Conventions embracing every part of the country.

The attitude of the masculine public towards
the proposed reform — if the press may be taken

as a fair index — was marked by hostility, indifference, and amusement. A Philadelphia paper represented with essential accuracy the sentiments of a great majority of women when it declared: "The ladies of Philadelphia, therefore, under the influence of the most serious 'sober second thoughts,' are resolved to sustain their rights as Wives, Belles, Virgins, and Mothers, and not as Women."

Here, manifestly, was a cause implying "uphill all the way." For leadership in it the first thirty years of Miss Anthony's life supplied an ideal training.

In the first place she had the advantage of deriving from her father, Daniel Anthony, the best inheritances of a New England Quaker, and what these meant in the way of stiffening the spirit of personal independence nobody who remembers the reception accorded to Quakers in early New England, and their response to it, needs to be reminded. Her father was of the more liberal wing of his sect, and married "out of meeting." His wife, Lucy Read, came of Baptist parents, so positive in their own convictions that when the father was swept in later life into the less rigid faith of Universalism the mother is said to have "worn the skin off her knees" praying for his return to the Baptist fold. Both the Anthonys and the Reads, with roots respectively in Portsmouth, Rhode Island, and Rehoboth, Massachusetts, had moved from eastern to western Massachusetts shortly before the Revolution. Susan Brownell Anthony, named for an aunt, Susan Anthony Brownell, was born at Adams, Massachusetts, in sight of Greylock Mountain, February 15, 1820, the second of her parents' eight children, six of whom grew to maturity. A deep and warm family affection, planted in Susan as a child, remained one of her strongest characteristics through life. No matter how completely she became immersed through later years in the work to which she gave herself, the call of her kindred in time of need took precedence of all other demands.

Daniel Anthony, her father, whose uncommon capacity and spirit admirably supplemented the gentle qualities of his wife, had the early benefit of a boarding-school training, followed by a short experience of teaching. With an enlarged mind he became one of the pioneer cotton manufacturers of his native region, from which he moved, with extended prospects in the same field, to Battensville, New York. Here, for more than ten years from 1826, he throve, with a general store besides his cotton mill. His strong temperance principles forbade the usual sale of drink in his store, which nevertheless had a considerable patronage. It was characteristic of the times that, although Daniel Anthony would not sell liquor, he kept in his house for the use of "high seat" Quakers, on their way to and from Quarterly Meeting, a liberal supply of tobacco, gin, and brandy, to which they helped themselves freely. More than once his "worldliness" in such directions as wearing clothes "out of plainness" got him into trouble with the Society of Friends. When he allowed the upper room of his house to be used for a dancing-school, — in which his daughters, be it said, were permitted no more than the rôle of spectators, — he was read, though very reluctantly, out of meeting. By this time, through the general business conditions which had their outward token in the panic of 1837, he had encountered serious financial difficulties, culminating in a New York village with the ill-omened name of Hardscrabble, changed through his influence as postmaster, but without advantage to his fortunes, to Central Falls. The final crash reduced him from comparative wealth to poverty such as he and his had never known. They managed, however, to acquire, in 1845, a small farm near Rochester, New York, and the head of the family took up, with a substantial measure of enduring success, the business of insurance in that city. The intense sympathy and support which he gave to all the interests of his daughter Susan, when she entered upon her own work in the world, made him indeed an essential part of her life.

Before reaching thirty she had undergone the training and manifested the qualities which determined her career. After attending a district school in Battensville, she was one of the pupils in the school her father established for his children and their neighbors in his own house. For all his prosperity he was glad to have his daughters, when they were old enough, begin to teach the younger children of the school — a proceeding which provoked criticism at a time when "females" who could help it were not expected to take up work that was worth paying for. The father's good sense in this respect bore its fruit in the dark decade of the family fortunes, when Susan's experience, supplemented by a year at a boarding-school near Philadelphia, qualified her for good positions as a school-teacher, the last and best of which was that of head of the Female Department of the Canajoharie (New York) Academy from 1846 to 1849.

While enjoying the satisfaction of adding

through this work to the family resources, Miss Anthony was passing through other maturing experiences. In one of her schools she had the traditional encounter with the "school bully," whom she succeeded in flogging after a hard fight. With other young men she met the more usual experiences of young womanhood. From one after another of them she received proposals of marriage, though never from one from whom it seems to have given her much pain to turn away. It is even recorded that in later life, when a widower who had once admired her sought to renew their acquaintance, she caused her secretary to answer his letter. It was no unwarranted flight of fancy for a rhymester, celebrating her fiftieth birthday, to produce, as one of many stanzas:

> She might have chose an honored name,
>   And none have scorned or hissed it;
> Have written Mrs. Jones or Smith,
>   But strange to say, she Missed it.

The pictures of her in the years before her appearance had taken on the severity and angularity associated with reformers represent a tall young woman by no means uncomely and with features clearly suggesting uncommon force of character. "Strong-minded" as she must have looked, she

SUSAN B. ANTHONY
EARLY AND LATE

followed her father quite far enough out of Quaker-
ism to acquire a healthy liking for pretty dresses.
When a brother-in-law, delighted with her capa-
cities as a cook, said, "I'd rather see a woman make
such biscuits than solve the knottiest problem in
algebra," she answered, "There is no reason why
she should not be able to do both." It is worth
remembering that throughout her life she liked to
practise her skill in cooking and to wear becoming
colors and clothes.

In one of her letters from boarding-school she
wrote home, "It is far easier for us to perceive
where others should reform than to observe and
correct our own imperfections, while perhaps our
failings are completely disgusting in the sight of
others." Among her failings she learned in later
years to count the labored manner of her writing.
"That has been the way all my life," she declared
on looking over some of her letters as a schoolgirl.
"Whenever I take a pen in hand I always seem to
be mounted on stilts." The reports of her early
speeches, delivered from manuscript, fully confirm
this self-imposed verdict. It was not long, however, before, gaining confidence, she trusted entirely to notes and headings in her public addresses,
and acquired the reputation of a most effective
speaker.

When she began to appear on public platforms, few women dared, or were even permitted, to let themselves be seen and heard in this way. Her very first speech, before the Daughters of Temperance in Canajoharie, was accomplished without difficulties. By this time — 1849 — she had lost all interest in teaching, and at the end of the school year went to help her father with his farm while he was building up his insurance business in Rochester near by. The household was a hotbed of liberal discussion, visited by Garrison, Wendell Phillips, W. H. Channing, Frederick Douglass, and many other reformers, especially in the antislavery field. All the surrounding influences drew Daniel Anthony's zealous and able daughter to the platform, though it was not yet ready to welcome her.

In 1852, as a Rochester delegate of the Daughters of Temperance, she attended a mass meeting of the Sons of Temperance at Albany, and learned with chagrin that "the sisters were not invited there to speak but to listen and learn." In the same year the appearance of women delegates, including Miss Anthony, as possible speakers at the Convention of the Men's Temperance Society at Syracuse caused a noisy commotion. Shouted down when she tried to speak, she took part in organizing a meeting of women to whom she delivered the address she had prepared for the mixed audience. The more conservative sentiment had indeed not changed greatly since the orthodox ministers of Massachusetts had issued in 1837 a Pastoral Letter, declaring, "We cannot, therefore, but regret the mistaken conduct of those who encourage females to bear an obtrusive and ostentatious part in measures of reform, and countenance any of that sex who so far forget themselves as to itinerate in the character of public lecturers and teachers."

But it was not long before her opportunity came to "score." In the summer of 1853 she attended a State Teachers' Convention at Rochester, and for most of two days sat silent while all the speaking was done by men, though two thirds of those present were women. At the end of the second day the subject, "Why the profession of teacher is not as much respected as that of lawyer, doctor, or minister," was under discussion. Miss Anthony then astonished the gathering by rising and saying, "Mr. President." "What will the lady have?" blandly asked the presiding officer. "I wish to speak on the question under discussion," she replied. The president's inquiry, "What is the pleasure of the Convention?" led to a half-hour's debate, through which Miss Anthony stood, fearing to lose the floor should she sit down. When it was finally voted that she should be heard, she said:

"It seems to me you fail to comprehend the cause of the disrespect of which you complain. Do you not see that so long as society says woman has not brains enough to be a doctor, lawyer, or minister, but has plenty to be a teacher, every man of you who condescends to teach tacitly admits before all Israel and the sun that he has no more brains than a woman?"

Many of the women in the convention were as much outraged by her performance as many of the men, but on the next day they adopted resolutions recognizing the right of female teachers to share in all the privileges and deliberations of the gathering and demanding the removal of existing discriminations against women teachers in the matter of salary. Miss Anthony had demonstrated impressively the power she was destined to exert.

Over and above the causes of temperance and the women teachers, the cause of antislavery was engaging the most ardent reformers of the day. Historically the rights of the Negro and of woman were closely linked as objects of reform. As early as 1840 this intimate relation manifested itself at a World's Antislavery Convention in London, to which a number of Americans, both men and women, went as accredited delegates. On their arrival they found that the women were not expected to speak. Indeed, after a heated debate they were relegated to seats fenced off by a bar and curtain, and when Garrison arrived too late to take part in the discussion leading to this course, he refused his seat in the convention and became a silent spectator in the gallery. Among the American women Lucretia Mott and Elizabeth Cady Stanton were deeply aggrieved, and resolved to educate the American public in justice towards women. The account of the whole matter in the official *History of Woman Suffrage* ends with the words: "The movement for woman suffrage, both in England and America, may be dated from this World's Antislavery Convention."

It was especially as an antislavery speaker, then, that Miss Anthony began to make herself felt. A little later than her father and other members of her family she came to feel the importance of promoting separately the cause of women. Attending her first Women's Rights Convention at Syracuse in 1852, she became one of the secretaries of the meeting. An editorial in the *New York*

Herald on this convention declared in one of its less coarsely scurrilous paragraphs:

> How did woman first become subject to man, as she now is all over the world? By her nature, her sex, just as the Negro is, and always will be to the end of time, inferior to the white race and, therefore, doomed to subjection, but she is happier than she would be in any other condition, just because it is the law of her nature.

As a favorite Abolitionist speaker, the Negress, "Sojourner Truth," said in this same year of 1852: "Well, chil'ern, whar dar is so much racket dar must be somet'ing out of kilter. I t'ink dat 'twixt de niggers of de Souf and de women at de Norf all a talkin' 'bout rights, de white man will be in a fix pretty soon."

From every angle the wrongs of Negroes and of women seemed to call upon spirits like Miss Anthony for righting. If the chief emphasis of her work through the fifties was upon antislavery agitation, it was as an item in a general programme of liberation. Her antislavery work reached its climax in the early months of 1861, between the election and inauguration of Lincoln, when, with other Abolitionists, she attempted to conduct a series of meetings in the cities and towns of New York to advocate "No compromise with Slaveholders. Immediate and Unconditional"

Emancipation." In the smaller communities, where there were not enough rowdies to make a mob, the meetings were held without difficulty. In such larger places as Buffalo, Syracuse, and Albany, the speakers encountered every form of opposition — cayenne pepper on the stove, jeers and groans, rotten eggs, the burning of effigies, including one of Miss Anthony herself. Through all this she stood her ground as the born fighter must, usually howled down, but bearing herself — if the similitude may be permitted — like a man.

We must not leave the fifties without recalling one episode of the Woman Movement in which Miss Anthony and some of her colleagues were thought to bear themselves entirely too much like men — in the wearing of "bloomers." This extremely modest bifurcated costume took its name from one of the group of early suffragists who adopted it, Mrs. Amelia Bloomer of Seneca Falls, New York, editor of a reform journal, *The Lily*. She does not really deserve the immortality of a Sandwich or a Boycott, since the costume owed its origin to Elizabeth Smith Miller, a daughter of Gerrit Smith and cousin of Elizabeth Cady Stanton. Yet Mrs. Bloomer stuck to it for eight years, whereas most of her sister dress-reformers gave out after about two — largely for

the sake of their own men-folk, who were subjected to unbearable ridicule when they appeared
in public with their oddly clad wives and sisters.
It was to the credit of these women that they
realized even so soon as they did that they were
hurting rather than helping their cause. Fantastic
as they seemed to their contemporaries, it has
remained for our own day to provide the spectacle
of a lady bathing at Atlantic City in a dress of
reasonable modesty, only to find herself in process
of "rescue" by the lifeguard, who thought she
had fallen into the water fully clothed.

When the Civil War began Miss Anthony was
frankly disappointed in the attitude of her fellow
Abolitionists and woman suffragists, who were
ready to give precedence to the preservation of
the Union over all other causes. "I have tried
hard to persuade myself," she wrote to a friend,
"that I alone remained mad, while all the rest
had become sane, because I have insisted that it
is our duty to bear not only our usual testimony
but one even louder and more earnest than ever
before. . . . I have not yet seen one good reason
for the abandonment of all our meetings, and am
more and more ashamed and sad that even the
little Apostolic number have yielded to the world's
motto — 'The end justifies the means.' "

APPEARANCE-OF A LADY IN THE NEW BLOOMER COSTUME.

FROM GLEASON'S "PICTORIAL DRAWING ROOM
COMPANION," AUGUST 9, 1851

Late in 1862 she was sadly shaken by the sudden death of her beloved father. A few months after this loss, feeling that she was carrying out what would have been his wish, she joined with Mrs. Stanton in calling a meeting in New York — May 14, 1863 — to organize the Women's National Loyal League, for the purpose of bringing the women of the country to the complete support of Lincoln and his policies. But those policies, as they pointed out in their resolutions and in an address to the President written by Mrs. Stanton and Miss Anthony, must look towards freedom for all — black and white, men and women. "We ask you now," they wrote to Lincoln, "to finish your work by declaring that nowhere under our national flag shall the motherhood of any race plead in vain for justice and protection."

To the work of this National Loyal League, in the organization of meetings and securing a vast number of signatures to petitions to Congress, Miss Anthony devoted herself with unflagging energy for more than a year. The black slave and the white woman were, in her eyes, so nearly on an equality of servitude that it is hard to say which of her two causes took the first place in her interest at the moment.

It was the Rev. W. H. Channing who first

called Miss Anthony "the Napoleon of the woman suffrage movement." But Napoleon had no twin brother in his leadership, as Miss Anthony had a twin sister in the person of Elizabeth Cady Stanton. The instance of their coöperation in the work of the Women's National Loyal League was but one out of many. Theodore Tilton once said of their partnership in effort: "I know of no two more pertinacious incendiaries in the whole country; nor will they themselves deny the charge. In fact, this noise-making twain are the two sticks of a drum for keeping up what Daniel Webster called 'the rub-a-dub of agitation.'" From the time of their first meeting in 1851 until Mrs. Stanton's death in 1902 these two women joined their complementary abilities for the achievement of their common purpose. Together they wrote innumerable resolutions, reports, and speeches — an enormous total product, including their combined labors on the first four of the six vast volumes of the *History of Woman Suffrage.*

To all this work Mrs. Stanton, the more radical, imaginative, and "cultivated" of the two, brought the greater capacity for happy expression, Miss Anthony, the more methodical and sure-footed, — who declared "I love to make history but hate to write it," — the richer arsenal of

ELIZABETH CADY STANTON

fact. "You stir up Susan," said Mrs. Stanton's husband to her one day, "and she stirs up the world." Susan, in fact, was quite capable of stirring up Mrs. Stanton — as when she wrote a letter that shamed her into crossing the Atlantic against her easy-going inclination. From Mrs. Stanton came the written warning, "Ah, beware, Susan, lest as you become 'respectable' you become conservative." Each indeed needed and responded to the stimulus which the other could provide, and the record of either would be incomplete without some record of the other.

To the passage of the Thirteenth Amendment in February, 1865, putting an end to slavery in the United States, Miss Anthony and Mrs. Stanton had every right to feel that the influence of the Women's National Loyal League had made some contribution. But this was not nearly enough to satisfy them. When the Thirteenth Amendment emancipated the Negro race, its members did not receive the right to vote. That came later in the Fifteenth, adopted in 1870. Meanwhile, in 1863, the Fourteenth, defining citizenship and the rights of representation, introduced the word "male" into the Constitution in a manner which filled the woman suffragists with disgust and alarm. Evidently the war had fallen far short of producing the general extension of privileges for which the women had been working — and again the fight was on.

It was not rendered an easier fight by the fact that most of the men who had been supporting the dual cause of antislavery and universal suffrage took the position that this was "the Negro's hour"; that one idea was enough for a generation; and that other reforms, including temperance, were more pressing than women's rights. This was not at all in accordance with Miss Anthony's view of the matter, and, after spending the greater part of 1865 with her brother Daniel in Kansas, where he was mayor of Leavenworth, she returned to the Eastern scene of action, full of vigor for the struggle which was to occupy the rest of her long life.

II

To follow the struggle in any detail would carry us far beyond the scope of this chapter. Much of the work in connection with it was a work of organization, especially in the planning and management of conventions, a form of administrative activity in which Miss Anthony was notably proficient. Through the fifties she had served her apprenticeship, in both antislavery and women's rights conventions. Immediately after the war she took an important part in the work of the American Equal Rights Association, organized to promote the right of suffrage irrespective of race, color, or sex. Then, in 1869, with suffrage clearly in sight for the Negro, came the formation of the National Woman Suffrage Association and, later in the same year, the American Woman Suffrage Association.

As in England the agitators of woman suffrage came to be known as "suffragists" and "suffragettes," — the advocates of less and more violent measures of reform, — so the American and the National Associations were distinguished here, and Miss Anthony found her natural affiliation in the National, the more radical of the two bodies. Gradually drawing together through twenty years, they united in 1889 as the National-American Woman Suffrage Association. Whether through the nature of their leadership, or because of differences of national temper, the suffragettes of America have never found it necessary to destroy works of art, chain themselves to iron gratings in a hall of legislation, or immolate themselves under the hoofs of a horse on the racetrack. The quality of leadership could not have been without its effect. Mrs. Stanton was president of the National and National-American Association, with Miss Anthony incessantly at her right hand, from 1869 to 1892. From 1892 to 1900 Miss Anthony herself held the presidency, retiring at eighty, to be succeeded by Mrs. Catt. The influence of "the Napoleon's" positive personality was an element of incalculable force in the history of the whole movement.

In addition to all her work of organization and direction, there was of course an enormous output of personal expression in speaking and letter-writing. There was even a brief experience of weekly journalism, under conditions not far from sensational. In 1867 she and Mrs. Stanton went to Kansas to put their shoulders to the wheel in a state campaign for woman suffrage — which met, for all their arduous travel and speech-making, with overwhelming defeat. It was at a time when they were sadly discouraged by what seemed to them the defection of the men who felt that the cause of women should just then give place to that of the Negro. Help from any quarter was welcome, and they accepted an offer of it from the eccentric George Francis Train. He joined them, in his evening clothes, on their speaking tour, and, after telling Miss Anthony casually one day that he would finance a woman suffrage paper for her, took away her breath by making a public announcement on the same evening:

"When Miss Anthony gets back to New York she is going to start a woman suffrage paper. Its name is going to be *The Revolution;* its motto, 'Men, their rights, and nothing more; women, their rights, and nothing less.' This paper is to be a weekly, price two dollars per year; its editors, Elizabeth Cady Stanton and Parker Pillsbury; its proprietor, Susan B. Anthony. Let everybody subscribe for it!"

Thus, all unexpectedly, she was in for it. Her old friends thought she was mad to embark on such an enterprise, and they were nearly right. Frankly radical in many directions, the paper, maintained at first by Train's money, lasted under Miss Anthony's management, from January, 1868, for a little more than two years. Train went to Ireland on the day of the first issue of *The Revolution*, got himself arrested for complicity with Fenians, and was imprisoned for a year in Dublin — the very name of the paper, copies of which were found in his possession, being taken as evidence of his guilt. The end was foreordained, and Miss Anthony was lucky finally to get off with a personal debt of no more than $10,000. For once her shrewd good-sense seems to have deserted her.

But she was not yet too old to profit from the painful experience.

Her frequent appearances in print and in person had made her by this time a widely known public figure. Any unusual display of her views attracted general attention, and in 1872 she displayed them in a striking fashion.

In suffrage circles it was plausibly argued that under the Fourteenth Amendment women were entitled to all the privileges of citizenship, among which the suffrage was to be counted. Miss Anthony, besides giving this theory wide currency through *The Revolution*, resolved to put it to the test. On November 1, 1872, after reading the exhortation of a Rochester paper that all voters should register for the approaching presidential election, and having fortified herself with what seemed sound legal advice, she persuaded the inspectors at the registry of voters to enroll her name for the balloting of four days later. The names of her younger sister Mary and other women were accepted at the same time. On election day the fifteen women registered in her ward succeeded in depositing their ballots. Within a few weeks Miss Anthony found herself arrested for illegal voting and under bail to appear before a United States Court for trial. She always regretted that through the gallantry of her counsel she was not permitted to refuse bail and go to prison — in which event she could have appealed to the Supreme Court on a writ of habeas corpus.

In the interval between her indictment and trial, from November to the following June, she went about making speeches calculated to strengthen her case before a jury — first in one county, then, on a change of venue, in another. The *History of Woman Suffrage* describes Judge Hunt, who tried the case, as "a small-brained, pale-faced, prim-looking man, enveloped in a faultless suit of black broadcloth, and a snowy white necktie." The account of the whole matter is written in an openly *ex parte* vein. It appears, however, that the bench, having heard the arguments for and against the defendant, declined to give the case to the jury, produced an opinion which he had written in advance, and directed a verdict of guilty. The fine of one hundred dollars and costs was never exacted. The case was much discussed in the press, often with severe condemnation of the judge. It is nevertheless significant that a unanimous decision of the United States Supreme Court on a similar case, delivered less than two years later by Chief Justice Waite, himself a believer in woman suffrage, vindicated the opinion of

Judge Hunt by declaring, in the light of recent amendments, that "the Constitution of the United States does not confer the right of suffrage upon anyone, and that the Constitutions and laws of the several States which commit that important trust to men alone are not necessarily void." This left Miss Anthony no alternative but to work thenceforth for a Sixteenth Amendment extending the suffrage to women — eventually reached as a Nineteenth — and for changes in the constitutions of the States. But the *History of Woman Suffrage* was probably well within the truth in its assertion that "the effect of Miss Anthony's prosecution, conviction, and sentence was in many ways advantageous to the cause of freedom. Her trial served to awaken thought, promote discussion, and compel an investigation of the principles of government."

Indeed her activities and those of her colleagues were counting in many ways. Long before the coming of woman suffrage — which they regarded as the very keystone of the arch of freedom — the discriminations against women as such were dropping one by one away. Colleges and universities throughout the land were receiving them on equal terms with men; in business and professional life the doors of opportunity were opening wider and wider; their property rights were firmly established. This could not have become an accomplished fact without a general change of sentiment towards the cause for which Miss Anthony stood — a change broad enough to include both cause and champion.

It is told of her that late in life she stood on a platform at the end of a speech in a large American city, almost knee-deep in the flowers rained upon her by enthusiastic hearers. "Time brings strange changes," she said. "In this very city that has pelted me with roses I have been pelted with rotten eggs for saying the very things that I have said to-night." At an earlier time a yellow dog had appeared on a Chicago platform while she was speaking and, rearing up, had laid his nose on her shoulder. "I prophesied to the audience then," she said afterwards, "that the dog would figure in the press reports more conspicuously than anything that was said or done, and so he did. He occupied half of the space in every paper." The hostility and levity that marked her earlier treatment by the public gave place by degrees to a far-spreading admiration and affection for the venerable lady who came to be known to the many as "Aunt Susan," or even — with a bold hagiologic suggestion — as "Saint Anthony."

The change of course implied the recognition of long-continued manifestations of character and ability. These were made in the eyes of the whole public — in campaigns throughout the country resulting gradually in the extension of woman suffrage, through municipal and other minor elections, to the broader fields covered by changes in State constitutions; in congressional hearings; in two visits to Europe, during the first of which, at Paris, in 1883 she had her first experience of breakfast in bed; in national woman suffrage conventions and other meetings. As she went about the land, encountering all manner of men and women, she left in many circles the impression produced upon Garrison's daughter Fanny, Mrs. Henry Villard, who wrote, apropos of the hundredth anniversary of Miss Anthony's birth: "I was immediately drawn to Miss Anthony as a child whenever she visited my parents and I watched her smiling face, so constantly full of fun and so illumined by a noble spirituality. A more thoughtful and considerate visitor never came into any home. Wherever she went, her ready sympathy and helpfulness inspired affection and made her a welcome guest."

As she grew very old, she began to suffer from limitations of her abounding physical strength.

Yet at eighty-five she gave no heed to the pro-
tests of friends who would have dissuaded her
from attending the National Suffrage Convention
in Portland, Oregon, in 1905, on the score that
she might die on the train. "It would make a
little more trouble for others," she declared, "but
I cannot give up going about my work for constant fear of that." The next year she attended
the annual Suffrage Convention — her last — at
Baltimore, in January 1906, and made a brief
address, ending with the words: "Most of those
who worked with me in the early years have
gone. I am here for a little time only and then my
place will be filled as theirs was filled. The fight
must not cease; you must see that it does not stop."
Before returning to her home in Rochester, she
appeared at a public celebration of her eighty-
sixth birthday in Washington on February 15.
At the end of an overwhelming evening she
spoke her last words in public: "There have been
others also just as true and devoted to the cause
— I wish I could name every one — but with
such women consecrating their lives, failure is
impossible."

Less than a month later, on March 13, 1906,
she died — her faithful sister Mary, a less conspicuous but equally dedicated worker in the

suffrage cause, beside her — in their house at Rochester.

III

More than once the *History of Woman Suffrage* — of which Miss Anthony and Mrs. Stanton, with the collaboration of Mrs. Matilda Joslyn Gage, produced the first four volumes, and Mrs. Ida Husted Harper the fifth and sixth — has been cited in these pages. It is an enormous repository of record and opinion, and is so amply supplemented by the *Life and Work of Susan B. Anthony*, in three large volumes by Mrs. Harper, that no investigator need fear any lack of material. His danger is rather that of losing himself in a tropical forest of luxuriant growth both overhead and underfoot. A "mere man" may question whether the feminine historians might not have served their own cause better had they cut away more of the trees, if only to make the forest visible. Or shall a more appropriate metaphor be suggested, in wishing for a more liberal use of that domestic utensil, the sieve?

But the subject, involving a wide range of tendencies and personal influences, is vast, and it it is little wonder that its chroniclers have been carried to appalling lengths. The very scale of Miss Anthony's identification with the suffrage cause requires gigantic measurements. For half a century she embodied the enterprise in America. In the twenty years since her death the world has witnessed radical changes in many particulars. It was nearly ripe for woman suffrage when the World War came. The political parties, long loath to recognize its claims, had crept slowly onward. In 1872 the suffragists got, instead of the plank they hoped for in the Republican platform, a so-called "splinter." In 1912 Theodore Roosevelt, an entirely theoretical friend of woman suffrage while in power, declared himself heartily for it as the Progressive candidate for the presidency. By 1916 all the parties reached the point of endorsing it in their platforms.

In England the participation of women in war work — including employment in munition factories where they were subject, under the laws of warfare, to enemy attack — broke down the argument that those who could not render essential service in time of national peril should not vote, and woman suffrage was adopted in Great Britain before it became a part of the American system of government. Here too the war hastened its coming, and Woodrow Wilson, the War President, recognizing the logic of a new situation, urged upon Congress the adoption of the Nineteenth

Amendment. It was passed by Congress in June, 1919, and on August 26, 1920, having been ratified by three quarters of the States, was proclaimed in effect.

The logic of the essential situation had long been with the woman suffragists. There were nevertheless rational men and women who honestly doubted whether, granting all the logic, political conditions would really be bettered by doubling the size of an electorate already of huge proportions. After only six years of trial it can hardly be said that those conditions have changed notably for the better or the worse. But who shall say that when a clearly defined issue is placed before the voters of the country — a great question of social justice, of international coöperation, of peace or war — the women will not tip the scales to the side of righteousness and mercy? That is surely what should be expected of them. Meanwhile let men and women alike remember what a woman suffragist, Dr. Mary Putnam Jacobi, wrote more than thirty years ago: "After all, the most important effect of the suffrage is psychological. The permanent consciousness of power for effective action, the knowledge that their own thoughts have an equal chance with those of any other person, in being carried out by one's own will —

this is what has always rendered the men of a
free state so energetic, so acutely intelligent, so
powerful."

Energetic, acutely intelligent, powerful — may
the women of a free state justify these epithets
more universally than their fathers, brothers,
sons, and husbands have yet succeeded in doing!

VII

THE ROAD UP FROM SLAVERY

FOR BOOKER T. WASHINGTON AND HIS PEOPLE

"THY people shall be my people": so, to an extent unknown in other races, says the possessor of any appreciable infusion of Negro blood to the ancestor, even of the third and fourth preceding generation, from whom that blood is derived. His separation from the rest of the American population is a matter not only of custom, but in Southern states, also of law. The native Indians — far less numerous, to be sure, than the Negroes — have presented no problems comparable with the Negro Problem. The amalgamation of European and other stocks has been rapid and general throughout the United States. Even as I write these words, I remind myself that a witness no more remote than my father used to relate the coming of the first Irishman to the New England town in which he and I were born, and to tell how the visitant was drummed, immediately and actually, out of the place. Ships that sailed from that very town bore their part in the slave-trade, which, however respectable in its day, has stained the name of state and people. The Irishman, drummed out of town, came back, and merged into the general problem of American life. The Negro is still with us — a problem by himself.

All this is at once patent and readily explicable. The introduction of the Negro into the country as a slave, his continuance, in rapidly growing numbers, in that estate, for more than two centuries, his enfranchisement resulting from a civil war, place him in a position entirely unique. After some sixty years of freedom — years that began with many misguided steps towards "reconstruction" — the wonder is not so much that he remains a problem, as that his advance, in many of the fields of citizenship and civilization, has been so marked.

If there was ever a cause that needed a champion, it has been that of the Negro. At a definite time in Booker Washington's life, he became the acknowledged "leader of his race." This was upon the death of Frederick Douglass, who had borne that unofficial title for many years. Both of these men were born slaves — Douglass early enough to gain his freedom by an actual escape from his owners. All the slaves were set free while Washington was still a mere boy, but the emancipation secured to him by his own lifetime of effort was something greater than a physical deliverance. It was his constant thought that in saving himself he must save others also. No more truly of the famous Master of Rugby than of Booker Washington could it be said:

> Therefore to thee it was given
> Many to save with thyself;
> And, at the end of the day,
> O faithful shepherd! to come,
> Bringing thy sheep in thy hand.

The story of this champion is therefore to a peculiar degree the story of his cause.

I

The first items to be recorded with regard to the usual subject of biography are the date and place of his birth, the names of his parents, and the backgrounds of inheritance. Although Booker Washington stands apart from nearly all eminent men in this particular, in that no such records are in existence, he stands with multitudes of his own race born in slavery. There were plantations on which the births of slave children were recorded. On others they were not, and on one of these Booker Washington was born. The opening words of *Up from Slavery*, that classic of autobiography, tell the stark story:

I was born a slave on a plantation in Franklin County, Virginia. I am not quite sure of the exact place or exact date of my birth, but at any rate I suspect I must have been born somewhere and at some time. As nearly as I have been able to learn, I was born near a cross-roads post-office called Hale's Ford, and the year was 1858 or 1859. I do not know the month or the day.

Of his mother, to whom he was devotedly attached, little is recorded but that she was a cook for the slaves on her master's plantation, went by the name of Jane, extended on occasion into Jane Ferguson, and that her master's name was Burroughs. Of his father Booker Washington wrote:

I do not even know his name. I have heard reports to the effect that he was a white man who lived on one of the nearby plantations. Whoever he was, I never heard of his taking the least interest in me or providing in any way for my rearing. But I do not find especial fault with him. He was simply an unfortunate victim of the institution which the nation unhappily had engrafted upon it at that time.

It was enough for the child of these parents to go through his earliest years with no name but "Booker." When he went to school and found that the other pupils had at least two "entitles," he calmly gave himself, in answer to the teacher's inquiry about his second name, the august designation of "Washington." Learning later that his mother had named him "Booker Taliaferro" while he was still a child, he took to himself the full name of "Booker Taliaferro Washington." It was a name and nothing more, and for that very reason one of those disadvantages which its bearer came to look upon as advantages. With no family record to sustain, but merely a personal name to make, Washington and his like in handicap and incentive have succeeded again and again in turning these gravest losses to gains. This he was so constantly doing through tact of word and deed that, however he may have relished recording Frederick Douglass's words about his marriage to a white wife, it is hard to imagine Washington expressing himself in corresponding terms. "I am strongly of the opinion," said Douglass to a large assemblage of white and colored hearers, "that you will want me to say something concerning my second marriage. I will tell you: My first wife, you see, was the color of my mother and my second wife, the color of my father. You see I wanted to be perfectly fair to both races."

Pleasantries of this sort were quite out of keeping with Washington's early contacts with life. It

was a grim and exacting business for a Negro boy
in the sixties and seventies to lift himself above
his fellows in the South, to find, or make, and to
use the opportunities for advancement that might
come to him. During the war, the husband of
young Booker's mother, a slave belonging to
another master, had drifted, through following
some Northern troops, into the Kanawha valley
of West Virginia, and thither — to the town of
Malden — the mother and her children, when the
war was done, made their difficult way over the
mountains. There were salt mines and furnaces
and coal mines at Malden, and in these the boy
and one of his brothers were set to work as children. This was before the day of Child Labor
laws, for white or black, and Booker's work
often began at four in the morning.

The marking of the number 18 on the salt-
barrels packed by his stepfather excited his curiosity about figures and letters, and soon he was
filled with a consuming desire to learn to read.
In this longing he had his mother's sympathy,
which found a practical expression in providing
him with a copy of Webster's "blue-back" spell-
ing-book. There was nobody at hand to tell
him what the letters meant, but somehow he
managed to master the alphabet. While this was

in process, a Negro boy who had learned to read came to the town — a place of poverty and squalor, previously without a single reading Negro. The spectacle of this interpreter of the newspaper to groups of eager listeners brought both envy and determination to one of them. Soon the boy's chance appeared to have come, when another Negro with some education, qualified to conduct a school for Negro children in Malden, came to the town and opened a door which Booker would have entered with the very first, but that his step-father, unwilling to spare the boy's earnings from the family resources, kept him at work. Tortured every day by the sight of luckier children on their way to and from school, this boy was not one to be shut so summarily out of the Promised Land. With the connivance of his mother, he made arrangements with the teacher for lessons at night, made better progress, as he thought, than the day pupils, and gained a belief in the possibilities of night schooling which fortified him later at Hampton and Tuskegee.

"I never rise to speak before an American audience," Frederick Douglass once declared, "without a feeling that my failure or success will bring harm or benefit to my whole race." It would be absurd to ascribe to Booker Washington in his

FREDERICK DOUGLASS

boyhood any such feeling that he was a representative of his people and that through him they
would rise or fall. Whatever may have come
later in this respect, it is nevertheless entirely
within reason to see in the young Washington a
typical embodiment of his race, both in what lay
behind him and in what might lie ahead. The
transition from the state of ignorance and poverty
in which the war left the liberated blacks to all
the possibilities of freedom was a change analogous
to coming up from a dark cellar into the sunlight.
Dazzled and inept, hurt as often as helped by
mistaken friends and disguised enemies, the victims of political intrigue, shunning the fire with
burnt fingers after such a calamity as the failure
of the Freedmen's Bank, into which they had been
encouraged to pour their savings, the Negroes
needed more than anything else the guidance of a
pathfinder emerging from their own ranks — one
who could lead quite as much through the example of attainable experience as through precept. In Booker Washington such a pathfinder
was at hand. With the merry heart that goes all
the day, the traditionally happy temperament of
his race, yet with the moral and essentially religious fervor that breeds a strong sense of responsibility, with the nature, moreover, that led

him often to say, "No man, either white or black, from North or from South, shall drag me down so low as to make me hate him," he displayed from the first qualities which would have distinguished him in any race. But his beginnings, the obstacles to be overcome on his way, the achievements to which he attained, were those peculiarly of the Negro. Beyond the obstacles at which we have already looked there were many more.

There is a lifelong challenge in the old saying, "Obstacles are things to be overcome." Booker Washington spoke to the same philosophical purpose, when, out of his own experience, he wrote thus of his race: "Paradoxical as it may seem, the difficulties that the Negro has met since emancipation have, in my opinion, not always, but on the whole, helped him more than they have hindered him." In his own case, the difficulties of securing opportunities for the schooling on which he set his heart in early boyhood were in themselves the sources of great educational advantage. At first he tried to combine going to school with working, before and after school hours, in the coal-mine. Then, for the better disposition of his time, he took employment in the house of a local magnate, whose wife had won the reputation of a hard taskmistress, and had dismissed

boy after boy as unsatisfactory. She had come to
West Virginia from Vermont with the strictest
Yankee notions of neatness, order, and honesty.
The new boy-of-all-work adopted her standards,
and, with immense profit to his own future, made
them his own. By this time he had heard of the
Hampton Normal and Agricultural Institute in
Virginia, an outgrowth of the earliest attempt,
begun at Fortress Monroe during the war by the
American Missionary Association, to educate the
Negro. At such places as Beaufort and Hilton
Head, South Carolina, Northern teachers had set
to work almost as early, and when the war was
ended, the Freedmen's Bureau and other agencies
went on planting Negro schools through the
South. But Hampton presented itself to the young
Washington as a concrete fact and, though five
hundred miles away, as a goal to be reached at
any cost. He was only thirteen or fourteen years
old when, in the autumn of 1872, he left Malden,
with pitifully little money in his pocket, to make
his way to Hampton.

The story of his journey, by rail, by stage, and
afoot, ill clothed and fed, shut out of inns because
of his color, sleeping for some nights under a
board-walk at Richmond, is an extraordinary little
Odyssey. At Richmond, some eight miles from

Hampton, his meagre funds were exhausted, but finding himself a job at unloading pig iron from a vessel at one of the wharves, he earned enough to land himself finally at the place of his dreams — with fifty cents in his pocket.

The travel-stained, hungry boy who presented himself for admission to the Institute must have looked anything but a promising candidate, and as he saw one applicant after another admitted before him, he needed all the courage he could summon. After hours of uncertainty, the head teacher, Miss Mary F. Mackie, luckily gave him just the chance he was best qualified to take. "The adjoining recitation-room," she said, "needs sweeping. Take the broom and sweep it." Like his mistress at Malden, Miss Mackie was, in Washington's words, "a Yankee woman who knew just where to look for dirt." Before her inspection of his work, however, he had swept the room three times, and four times had applied the dust-cloth to woodwork, benches, tables, and desks. He had moved every piece of furniture and cleaned every closet and corner. After Miss Mackie had completed her scrutiny, and poked her handkerchief into all corners without finding a speck of dust, she declared, like a true Yankee, "I guess you will do to enter this institution."

More than once in recent times a group of students at Hampton has produced a dramatized representation of Booker Washington's entrance examination. George Herbert could have asked no more significant illustration of the servant who "makes drudgery divine," or of the truth behind his lines,

> Who sweeps a room, as for Thy laws,
> Makes that and th' action fine.

These early incidents are narrated in some detail, not to set the scale for what must follow, but merely to typify the spirit in which Washington went on from such beginnings. His entrance examination won him immediately a janitor's job which he held throughout his three years at the school. Through working, besides, in summertime as a waiter, through hard-earned help from a brother whom he prepared later for Hampton, and with assistance from a Northern friend of the school, he managed to meet the modest expenses of his education. Many things he learned — the beneficent uses of bath and toothbrush, the value of the Bible both as literature and as a help in living, the mastery of public speech. Most of all, he profited from intimate contact with the first principal of Hampton Institute, General S. C.

Armstrong, whom he described in later life as "the rarest, strongest, and most beautiful character that it has ever been my privilege to meet." From this potent advocate and formulator of the principle that the best all-round education of the Negro calls for the training of both hand and head, Booker Washington took the torch which he was destined to pass on for the illumination not only of his own race but of the cause of industrial education in general.

At his graduation from Hampton in June 1875, Washington was on the honor roll of commencement speakers. His funds were then so low that he was glad to find a place as waiter in a Connecticut summer hotel. It is tantalizing to lack all record of the impression he made — still a mere boy — upon the fashionable guests to whom he displayed such awkwardness as a waiter that he was reduced for a time to the lowlier post of dish-carrier. Much more in his element he found himself in the autumn, when he was chosen to teach the colored school in Malden. Here he had the satisfaction of preparing a number of pupils to enter Hampton, among them the generous older brother John, with whose help their adopted brother James was also sent to Hampton — both to become associated later with his own work at

Tuskegee. After two years of this teaching at Malden — with the bath and toothbrush zealously included as elements of education — came eight months of profitable study at the Wayland Seminary in Washington, attended by more prosperous Negroes not in search of industrial training. The experience tended to confirm his belief in schools of the Hampton type, as contributing more to a sense of self-dependence.

In himself this sense was strengthened by an invitation to return to West Virginia and take the stump as a political speaker on behalf of choosing Charleston, only five miles from Malden, as the capital of the State. This he did with marked success, and immediately received the further encouragement of a request to deliver the postgraduate address at the Hampton Commencement of 1879, an invitation immediately followed by the offer of a place on the teaching staff at Hampton, with special duties as "house father" to the young Indians with whom the Government was beginning the experiment of Eastern education, and with provision for supplementary studies of his own.

Here, for a young man hardly more than twenty, was an opportunity for ripening development of the first value. Booker Washington, keen of mind and spirit, eager to go forward and already jealous that others should go with him, seized it to the full. The result was that when two years later, in 1881, an inquiry came to Hampton from Alabama about a suitable person, presumably white, to take charge of a Negro normal school about to be opened in the town of Tuskegee, General Armstrong asked Booker Washington whether he thought he could fill the place, was told that he would be willing to try, communicated with the inquirers from Tuskegee, and soon received a telegram reading, in effect, "Booker T. Washington will suit us. Send him at once."

What he found when he went from the well-equipped Hampton to Tuskegee in June of 1881 was nothing more than the assurance of an annual appropriation of $2000 from the Alabama Legislature. And this was entirely for teaching. Not a building, or any means for erecting one, was in sight. The very origin of the enterprise had its discouraging aspects. A white politician and former slaveholder had bargained for the Negro vote with a former slave by promising to secure State funds for a Negro school at Tuskegee — which he did, only to make for himself the name of "nigger-lover" and thus to lose the white vote and to terminate his political career. But he provided Booker Washington with the greatest of his advantageous obstacles in the form of what his biographers have well called a "landless, buildingless, teacherless, and studentless institution of learning."

Washington's first task was to find a schoolhouse and to strengthen local sentiment for the support of the school. He had no fear of lacking pupils when he could open his doors. The schoolhouse presented itself in the form of a shanty with so leaky a roof that on rainy days one pupil had to hold an umbrella over the teacher's head while other pupils recited their lessons. This was a tangible difficulty to be conquered. The intangible obstacles were those of prejudice against the whole undertaking. Negroes suspected that a teacher without a "Reverend" before his name must be a godless man. Among the surrounding whites there were many holding an instinctive sympathy with the Southern Senator who opposed all Negro education on the ground that "as soon as one nigger has learned anything he can go and hide behind the stumps and whisper it to another." Even at the North it was less than half a century since the people of Canterbury, Connecticut, had fired and mobbed the boarding-school for girls in which Prudence Crandall ventured to receive colored pupils; and at Canaan, New Hampshire, where the local academy had admitted Negro boys, a committee of the town meeting carried out its order to "remove" the school, employing for that purpose some three hundred persons and a hundred yoke of oxen. These were instances of attempts at equal treatment for black and white. At Tuskegee there was of course no such question of combining the races, even as at Hampton, in the capacity of teachers and taught. Nevertheless, the sympathy of both races had to be won, if the experiment was to succeed.

The difficulties at first were portentous. As Washington went about the neighboring country to make the school known to the people he wanted to reach, he encountered appalling conditions — whole families sleeping in one-room cabins, eating miserable food, in one case with a single fork for five persons, though a sixty-dollar organ, in process of purchase on the installment plan, occupied a corner of the room. It was from just such cabins, however, that he secured his first recruits for the school, which was opened, July 4, 1881, with thirty pupils, male and female. Some of them had already been teachers, and were imbued with the idea that manual labor was a little beneath their dignity. All that Washington had learned at

Hampton about industrial training was confirmed by his discovery of the crying need for it, revealed in the study of his problem in Alabama. Accordingly, he made it a cardinal principle that any work to be done about the school should be done by the pupils themselves. The opportunities came thick and fast upon the early purchase, with five hundred dollars borrowed on his own responsibility and punctually repaid, of a plantation near Tuskegee, with a dilapidated mansion-house and other buildings suited to school use. When a bit of woodland needed to be cleared, he organized a "chopping-bee," and worked so hard and well with his own axe that the doubtful ones were shamed into emulating him. When further building became possible, he met and conquered extreme difficulties in the way of establishing a brick-kiln and teaching his pupils both to make and to lay bricks. In every way he emphasized the dignity of labor. The principle of the thing was well put in his later words:

There is just as much that is interesting, strange, mysterious, and wonderful, just as much to be learned that is edifying, broadening, and refining in a cabbage as there is in a page of Latin. There is, however, this distinction: It will make very little difference to the world whether one Negro boy, more or less, learns to construe a page of Latin.

On the other hand, as soon as one Negro boy has been taught to apply thought and study and ideas to the growing of cabbages, he has started a process which, if it goes on and continues, will eventually transform the whole face of things as they exist in the South to-day.

In another place he drew a sharp distinction between labor under slavery and in freedom: "There is a vast difference between working and being worked. Being worked means degradation; working means civilization." Thus, for him, it became the object of Tuskegee "to teach our students to lift labor out of drudgery and to place it on a plane where it would become attractive, and where it would be something to be sought rather than something to be dreaded and if possible avoided."

From the humble beginnings of 1881 the Tuskegee Institute has grown into a vast institution of many departments, enrolling, at the time of Washington's death in 1915, some eighteen hundred students, with a corporate property valued at $2,000,000 and with forty-seven trades taught in a hundred buildings on more than two thousand acres of land. The steps in this extraordinary progress, the growth of the confidence on which it was built, would make a story far exceeding the present bounds. The amazing record is in large measure a demonstration of one man's character and ability. If he was fortunate in his helpers, that was because he deserved them. Among these, General Armstrong held a high place. On one occasion, they were on the very point of setting forth on a money-raising trip to the North together, accompanied by a quartette of Hampton singers, when Washington learned for the first time that all the meetings were to be in the interest of Tuskegee, and had reason to suspect that this was Armstrong's way of introducing him to Northern sources of support.

Washington was fortunate also in his marriages, of which he made three. His first wife, Fannie N. Smith of Malden, West Virginia, a Hampton graduate, lived less than two years as Mrs. Washington, leaving behind her, in 1884, an infant daughter, Portia. In 1885 he married Olivia A. Davidson, a native of Ohio, a graduate both of Hampton and of the Massachusetts State Normal School at Framingham, who came to Tuskegee only six weeks after the school began as Washington's first fellow teacher. Two sons were born of this marriage. So nearly white herself that her Negro blood might have passed unsuspected, the second Mrs. Washington claimed her African inheritance as confidently as Major Moton, the present principal of Tuskegee, of unmixed African descent, when he declared, "The white man can beat me at being a white man, but I can beat him at being a Negro." Miss Davidson, before and after her marriage to Washington, attracted much financial support to Tuskegee. She died in 1889, and in 1893 Washington married the wife who survived him, Margaret James Murray, a graduate of Fisk University, and lady principal of Tuskegee at the time of her marriage.

"Whatever may be the disadvantages and inconveniences of my race in America," Major Moton has also declared, in terms that clarify the understanding of men like himself and Booker Washington, "I would rather be a Negro in the United States than anybody else in any other country in the world." In the case of Washington, a domestic life of great happiness contributed largely to such contentment with his lot. Devoted to his family circle at Tuskegee, to his garden, his live stock, and pets, it was at home that he found what he called his "most solid rest and recreation." Throughout the country, meanwhile, his rare abilities as a public speaker, his invariable demonstrations of sincerity, good will, and wisdom, won for him a repute and recognition, even during the formative years of Tuskegee, which presaged the high place he was to occupy in American life.

II

It has been said that at a definite point — namely, on the death of Frederick Douglass — Booker Washington stepped into the position of leader of his race. This is almost literally true. Douglass died February 2, 1895. On September 18, 1895, Washington appeared, on the invitation of the Directors of the Atlanta Cotton States and International Exposition, as the speaker representing the Negro race at the ceremonies by which the Exposition was opened. It was a notable opportunity to address at one time influential representatives of the three elements in the national community which he was constantly trying to bring into a relation of mutual understanding — the Southern whites, the Northern whites, and the members of his own race. He seized his opportunity in a manner which changed his status in fifteen minutes from that — to employ his own words — of "merely a Negro school-teacher in a rather obscure industrial school" to that of a national leader.

The speech was the very model of what such a speech should be — simple, forcible, and eloquent, charged with the sincerity and good sense which mark the highest statesmanship. When at one point he raised his right hand, with fingers spread apart, and declared, "In all things that are purely social we can be as separate as the fingers, yet one as the hand in all things essential to mutual progress," the audience abandoned itself to frantic expressions of approval. At the end of the speech, Governor Bullock of Georgia crossed the platform and in the eyes of the great audience shook the orator's hand with a heartiness which must have prepared him in some measure for the letter that came soon afterwards from President Cleveland, saying, with other commendations of the address, "I think the Exposition would be fully justified if it did not do more than furnish the opportunity for its delivery." For other consequences of his triumph Washington must have been less prepared — among them, an offer from a Western newspaper to report an impending prize-fight for one thousand dollars and all expenses.

For all the tact and wisdom of which Booker Washington was capable in urging his belief that Negro education should concern itself with the hand as much as with the head, it was of course inevitable that he should encounter opposition, even from his own people. To the criticism provoked by the methods pursued at Tuskegee, the work of Hampton Institute was equally open. Major Moton has told of a Negro minister visiting

Hampton and objecting to the institution, in spite of its physical beauties, on the ground that "General Armstrong and his corps of workers were teaching the Negroes to be hewers of wood and drawers of water, and that at bottom he was training the Negro boys and girls to be servants to the white race: that he never saw a more beautiful campus, but that it was in his judgment a 'literary penitentiary.'"

This was an open expression of the feeling that has run high in the class of Negro intellectuals, defined by its brilliant member, Dr. W. E. Burghardt DuBois, as "the talented tenth." More than twenty years ago, he wrote: "The Negro race, like all races, is going to be saved by its exceptional men. The problem of education, then, among Negroes, must first of all deal with the Talented Tenth; it is the problem of developing the Best of this race that they may guide the Mass away from the contamination and death of the Worst, in their own and other races."

Amid all the conflict of opinion regarding the relative value of industrial and so-called higher education for the Negro race, what has actually happened is that establishments for training in both these directions have multiplied and thriven exceedingly. Washington himself was a trustee both of Fisk and of Howard University, and constantly sought graduates of such institutions as teachers at Tuskegee. If it happened that the leader of his race was identified with the manual side of Negro education, we may nevertheless be sure that he would have hailed as a fellow worker a leader of equal force in the more traditionally academic field, for he was a faithful student of the Bible, and must have valued that wisest of sayings, "These ought ye to have done, and not to leave the other undone." Yet in his lifetime the winds of conflict among his own people blew fiercely about him.

They were never more violent than on one occasion in the very Boston where Garrison and the early abolitionists had undergone the perils of popular disfavor. When a meeting of the Negro Business Men's League was to be addressed in July 1903, by Booker Washington, a group of Boston Negroes, angered by his apparent condoning of political and social injustice against their race, determined to break up the meeting. Warned in advance, the minister of the church on Columbus Avenue in which the gathering took place discovered that the conspirators had distributed cayenne pepper about the pulpit. Worse was to follow. When Washington rose to speak, a disturber of the peace cried out, "We don't want to hear you, Booker Washington! We don't like you. Your views and aims are not those with which we sympathize or think best for our race." Then came police intervention, the drawing — and plying — of a hatpin by an enraged woman and of a razor by a man, with consequent bloodshed. Washington finally accomplished his speech, and after it made a newspaper statement that ended: "The men who disturbed the meeting have found that an easy way to get their names into the newspapers and to secure a little notoriety which they could not otherwise obtain." Such, in large measure, was indeed the case. The presiding officer, a Negro prominent in political life, came later to declare, "I thought, as a young man, that Latin conquers everything. Washington read it right; Labor conquers all."

Though symptomatic of a widespread antagonism, in a fraction of the Negro population, to the theories which Hampton and Tuskegee put into practice, this disturbance was merely a local affair. Not so the commotion which followed Booker Washington's acceptance of President Roosevelt's invitation to break bread with him at the White House. There are differing versions of the story. Only two need be given here. In the biography by

Washington's secretary, Rev. Emmett J. Scott, and Mr. Lyman Beecher Stowe, it is told that Washington had been summoned one morning in 1901 to the White House to discuss with the President, who greatly valued his counsel, certain political appointments about to be made in the South; that since the discussion could not be completed at one sitting, the President asked Washington to return at dinner-time and continue it at the table and afterward — which he did. In *My Larger Education* Washington himself says that, on his arrival from the South for the desired interview, he found at the house of a colored friend with whom he was to stay an invitation from the President to dine that night at the White House, and that he did so, in company with the Roosevelt family and a gentleman from Colorado. That night he took train to New York, and the next morning noticed in one of the papers an obscure item about himself as a guest at the White House.

All might have gone forward as quietly as the incident itself, had not the same item in a Washington paper attracted the notice of the correspondent of a Southern journal, who seized upon it as the basis for a front-page scare-head communication. The Southern press took it up with resounding outcries against the two men, immediately charged

with conspiracy to tear down the social barriers
between the races. Both became the objects of
violent abuse, even to the point of threats against
their lives. Indeed, it became known later that
an assassin was hired by residents of Louisiana
to visit Tuskegee and kill Booker Washington.

Through all the turmoil both Roosevelt and
Washington remained silent. Ten years later
Washington wrote, in *My Larger Education:*

The public interest aroused by this dinner seemed all the
more extraordinary and uncalled for because, on previous
occasions, I had taken tea with Queen Victoria at Windsor
Castle; I had dined with the Governors of nearly every state
in the North; I had dined in the same room with President
McKinley at Chicago at the Peace Jubilee dinner; and I had
dined with Ex-President Harrison in Paris, and with many
other prominent men.

Nothing could suggest more clearly than this
affair the extreme thinness of the ice on which
Washington was constantly obliged to make his
way, especially in his relations with the Southern
whites. It bears testimony to the wisdom and
efficacy of his course in seeking always to conform
with the social customs of the section or country
in which he found himself that the full record of
his experiences as an incessant traveler, constantly

in hotels and trains, is so innocent of items of awkwardness to himself or to others.

The simple fact is that there was a largeness both in his aims and in the processes by which he fulfilled them that relegated small things to obscure places. There was a prophetic sentence in that early postgraduate address at Hampton of which some mention has been made. His topic was "The Force that Wins," and he characterized it in these terms: "It requires not education merely, but also wisdom and common sense, a heart set on the right, and a trust in God." These are the qualities which his whole life exemplified.

It was a life spent, like Saint Paul's, "in journeyings often." Up and down the land, North and South, he traveled, winning financial support for his school not only from individual contributors of varying capacity to give, but also from the administrators of funds and foundations, who learned more and more that his work was a piece of national service which they must further; winning also the confidence of the three classes he set out to influence, the whites at the South and at the North, and Negroes of all sections. This he achieved in largest measure through the exercise of his great gift of oratory. A life of single purpose stood effectually behind it; but as he appeared before the public he brought to bear upon multitudes of hearers and readers the great power of clear thinking, direct expression, the employment of homely and humorous illustrations, such as stories in the dialect of his people, and over and above all, a pervading earnestness and sincerity.

It was a life, moreover, calling for the constant outpouring of physical strength. For more than forty years, from the time of his entering Hampton in 1872, he spent that strength, of which he had a plentiful endowment, without stint. At length it became necessary for a nurse to accompany him on his speaking tours and to provide him with a special diet. In spite of these precautions, he suffered several complete collapses. In the summer of 1915, defying all warnings of increasing weakness, he conducted in Boston a meeting of the National Negro Business League, of which he was the president and founder, and later kept his appointment to make an address before the Negro National Baptist Convention in Chicago. In the autumn the trustees of Tuskegee in New York insisted, after a final collapse, on his going to St. Luke's Hospital in that city for treatment. One of the doctors who examined him declared that it was "uncanny to see a man up and about who ought by all the laws of nature to be dead." When he was told that he had but a few days to live, he announced his intention of starting at once for home. "I was born in the South," he declared, "I have lived and labored in the South, and I expect to die and be buried in the South." So, in weakness and eagerness, he set out on the long journey to Tuskegee, and there he died, November 14, 1915, on the very morning after his arrival.

His life had dramatized the possibilities of a race. Irrespective of race, it had also enriched the annals of his country with a figure of genuine greatness — the greatness of a true patriot and of an essential gentleman. "History will tell us of two Washingtons," said Andrew Carnegie, "one white, the other black, both fathers of their peoples." From North and South, from black and white, from men of high and low estate, came at his death — as there has continued to come through the years that have intervened — a flood of testimony to his extraordinary powers and achievements. Of the many terms that have been coined to define him, "a Christian philosopher" conveys a vital element of the truth about him. Nearly seven years after his life ended, a statue commemorating the man and his work was unveiled at Tuskegee, a memorial secured entirely

THE BOOKER T. WASHINGTON MONUMENT
AT TUSKEGEE, BY CHARLES KECK

by the subscriptions of Negroes. In the ceremonies marking the occasion, the symbolism of transition from an old era to a new took visible form in the person of an aged Negro minister stretching trembling hands of benediction over a vast assemblage. He had begun his life as a slave in the family of Jefferson Davis.

If the theory of Mr. DuBois — that a race is saved by its exceptional men — be sound, the salvation of the Negro race cannot be more surely found than in the production of more men such as Booker Washington. But they are the exceptions in any race, as he would have been if his mother, like his father, had been white. If it is asked whether in this very mixture of blood some of his qualities may not have had their origin, there is the answer that both at Tuskegee and at Hampton, through a long term of years, the highest scholastic honors have been divided about equally between Negroes of mixed and unmixed African ancestry, and this in spite of the fact that in these schools the mixed have been in the majority. No, it is only fair to regard Washington as a true, if quite exceptional, representative of his people.

No single figure has taken the place he held as leader of his people. At the schools with which he was identified, and at many others in the South, the work to which he devoted his life goes valiantly on. Since his death, the group which opposed him has, in the words of Dean Kelly Miller of Howard University, "gained the ascendancy in dominating the thought and opinion of the race, but has not been able to realize to the least degree the rights and recognition so vehemently demanded." The industrial opportunities of the war-time brought half a million Negroes from the South to the North, without solving the racial problem in either section. The revival of the Ku Klux spirit — of which Washington thought he had seen the end in his early manhood — has contributed nothing more to the long-sought solution. Yet with all the discouragements, the future holds many signs of hope.

Where and why? Let the skeptic look at a recent issue of the *Negro Year Book*, setting forth the contemporaneous record of the race in business, industry, agriculture, education, and the arts. Let him remember the conditions of the race when its progress up from slavery began. Then leave him to his own conclusions.

SWORDS, PLOUGHSHARES, AND
WOODROW WILSON

WHETHER the prophet Micah was quoting Isaiah, or vice versa, or whether each was quoting an earlier prophet, there is no question that somebody set a long train of quotations in motion when he wrote, "And they shall beat their swords into ploughshares, and their spears into pruninghooks." One would hesitate to join that procession at so late a day as this but for the sake of recording the somewhat unfamiliar fact that about fifty years ago the prophecy had a strictly literal fulfillment. At the time of the Centennial Exhibition in Philadelphia the Universal Peace Union held a five days' meeting in Philadelphia, issued a declaration of peace to all mankind, and became the background of an episode that should be rescued from oblivion. "At this memorable gathering" — it is written in an official synopsis of the work of this organization — "several swords were presented to the Universal Peace Union by army officers who had carried them in battles. They were turned into a plough and pruninghooks, which were sent to the Paris Exposition of 1878, and afterward presented to the city of Geneva, and the plough now rests on a dais in the immortal hall where the Alabama question was settled."

There is a naïveté about this and other manifestations of workers for the suppression of war as the means of settling disputes between nations that has made many who are perfectly willing to subscribe to the beatitude, "Blessed are the peacemakers," unwilling to follow it with anything but "Cursed be the pacifists." This word — which in its form of "pacificists," now rarely heard, came nearer to an exact translation of peacemakers — was virtually a fighting word in wartime. Through connoting something akin to giving aid and comfort to the enemy, it became in many quarters — and it is not difficult to see why — a term of bitter reproach. Other words, good and bad, have similarly been bent from their true meaning. "Bolshevist" has in some measure supplanted "liberal"; and at the Chicago convention which nominated Harding another candidate was brought forward with the climax of encomium that he was "a man of ideals, but not an idealist," as if such a one were to be shunned like a leper. The extent to which the advocates of organized peace have fallen under the same condemnation is suggested by the words of Theodore Roosevelt, winner of the Peace Prize established by the inventor of dynamite: "All the actions of the ultrapacificists for a generation past, all their peace congresses and peace conventions, have amounted to precisely nothing in advancing the cause of peace."

The "ultrapacificists" — such men and women as those who led an early American peace agitator to exclaim, "There is such a thing as going beyond the millennium" — have indeed done many foolish things. At the same time they have steadily, through more than a century, nourished a sentiment which culminated at the Paris Peace Conference, primarily through the efforts of Woodrow Wilson, in the creation of the League of Nations. Before Wilson was born the general project of a Congress and Court of Nations was known in Europe as "the American plan." Its inception and furtherance were identical with ideals and personalities peculiarly American. The record of it all is a significant chapter in the annals of American causes. Whatever may be the ultimate relation of the United States to the League of Nations, a relation of direct or indirect blessing or bane, the cause of which the League is the embodiment has had so many American champions, chiefly effective among them all an American President who gave his life for it, that this book must needs include some consideration of the subject.

I

Let it be remarked at once that wars have always served to breed plans for peace. It may even be said, the greater the war the greater the plan. After the end of the Napoleonic wars, a strong but diffused sentiment that was concentrated in Benjamin Franklin's reiterated saying, "There never was a good war or a bad peace," began to express itself in writings, speeches, and concerted efforts of the like-minded. At the end of the World War the scattered plans of a century and more were codified, with many eliminations and elaborations, in the Covenant of the League of Nations. This document, received as something utterly novel and startling, was in fact the realization of the hopes and designs of generous, far-seeing spirits working through a long past towards a future in which wars may yet go the way of duels.

Through many centuries of history the state of war was the normal state of human existence. The mediæval Truce of God was merely a device to limit bloodshed by making festivals and holy days "closed seasons" for killing. As time went on such men as Erasmus, Henry IV of France, — in his "Grand Design," — Grotius, and Immanuel Kant went much further in seeking means to render peace more nearly permanent and wars less savage. It was always war that made men think of peace. When William Penn, in 1693, suggested an ambitious project of international arbitration in his "Essay towards the Present and Future Peace of Europe," — at the moment when the French, British, and other European armies were trying their best to destroy each other, — he exclaimed, "He must not be a man but a statue of brass or stone whose bowels do not melt when he beholds the bloody tragedies of this war." Many Americans in 1918 were using almost precisely these words.

They were doubtless also in frequent use during the wars with which the eighteenth century ended and the nineteenth began. It was in the course of these wars that what has come to be known as the Peace Movement had its origin in America, where the first peace society in the world was established some months before the second of its kind began its work in England. The full story of the movement, as a vehicle for the nurture and extension of ideas, would carry one far afield, into many lands. Here it is to be considered chiefly in its American — which, as it happens, has probably been its most significant — aspect.

One advantage of looking at the origin and early history of the peace movement in the United States lies in the resulting reminder that its primary impulse was religious rather than political. It was, and always has been, an attempt to apply to international relations some of the fundamental principles of the Christian religion. Its progress, like that of other religious principles, has been slow and intermittent; and the arrests in the movement forward have occurred when political considerations have ruled the day.

The founder of the first peace society in the world, David Low Dodge, of New York, was the very embodiment of the religious spirit that has actuated so many of the chief agitators for permanent peace. Born at Pomfret, Connecticut, in 1774, of sound Yankee and Calvinistic stock, old enough by the end of the Revolutionary War to have comprehended the havoc it wrought in his own domestic circle, turning as a young man from school-teaching to trade and commerce, which on his removal from Connecticut to New York he prosecuted with notable success, he became a

leader in the religious and business life of his time
and place. He established, besides, a family tradition of public usefulness, carried into the present
by his great-grandson, Mr. Cleveland H. Dodge,
of New York, a Princeton classmate and lifelong
friend of Woodrow Wilson.

It was significant of the intensity of Dodge's
religious feeling that his deep knowledge of the
Bible rested on his reading it critically from beginning to end forty-two times. In two pamphlets,
The Mediator's Kingdom Not of This World, published in 1809, and *War Inconsistent with the
Religion of Jesus Christ* (1812), this ardent Presbyterian went as far as any Quaker nonresistant
in condemnation even of wars of self-defense —
much farther than most of the New England advocates of peace who entered the field soon after
him. Though his second and more important
pamphlet was published while the War of 1812
was in progress, he and his coterie of sympathizers
in New York saw the wisdom of deferring the
establishment of a society to promote their views
until that war was ended. Accordingly in August
1815, the New York Peace Society, made up of
thirty or forty members, "wholly confined to
decided evangelical Christians, with a view to
diffusing peace principles in the churches, avoiding

all party questions," came into existence, and
began to circulate the writings of Dodge and
others who were soon writing to the same
purpose.

It was in December of the same year that the
Massachusetts Peace Society was formed. Like
many such organizations, it had a list of officers
including names of local dignity and fame, but
relied chiefly for its activities upon a single en-
thusiast. This was the Rev. Noah Worcester, a
prolific writer under the pseudonym, "Philo Pacificus," and for some time corresponding secretary
of the Massachusetts Peace Society, and editor of
its journal, *The Friend of Peace*. He was, besides,
one of the early Unitarian dissenters from the
orthodox Congregationalism of New England. A
memoir of him is to be found in an unexpected
place — a little volume with the title, *Lives of
Distinguished Shoemakers*. Worcester is included in
it by virtue of his having eked out his living as a
young minister with a growing family at Plymouth, Massachusetts, by shoemaking. "He made
a study of his shop, and a table of his lapboard."
This was immediately after the War of the Revolution, in which he had taken a boy's part at
Bunker Hill and Bennington. Not until 1814,
when he was nearing sixty years of age, did he

produce a pamphlet embodying his vigorous feeling against the institution of war and destined, through its translation into many languages, to make his name known far beyond his native land. The pamphlet was called, in full, *A Solemn Review of the Custom of War, Showing that War is the Effect of Popular Delusion, and Proposing a Remedy*. Though not, like Dodge's writings, including defensive war in its condemnations, its note was struck by the repeated query, "Shall the sword devour forever?" In proposing a remedy — as if in early prophecy of the League of Nations and the World Court — Worcester asked: "But if the eyes of people could be opened in regard to the evils and delusions of war, would it not be easy to form a confederacy of nations, and organize a high court of equity, to decide national controversies?" It was the chief object of Worcester, who came to be called the "Apostle of Peace," to open the eyes of his contemporaries. With what diligence he set himself to this end may be gathered from his own words spoken some eight years after the publication of his "Solemn Review" — which appeared, by the way, almost simultaneously with the signing of the Treaty of Ghent: "I believe I may say with truth that, when awake, the subject of war has not been absent from my mind an hour at a time in the whole course of the eight years." When asleep, such a devotee would have been dreaming of his subject.

If the Apostles of Peace are to appear in an apostolic succession, the name of William Ladd of Portsmouth, New Hampshire, and Minot, Maine, should follow immediately upon that of Noah Worcester. Ladd, a native of Exeter, and a graduate of Harvard College in the class of 1797, began his life as a sailor on the ships of his father, a Portsmouth merchant. He became a skillful navigator, and before the War of 1812 commanded vessels of his own. When the American merchant marine was driven from the sea, Ladd left it also, but never to return. He used to say, "The knowledge which I gained in college the salt water washed out of my memory." But the sea taught him other things, among them the advantages of concentration upon a single object: it was the sailor in him that answered, in declining an invitation to speak on temperance, "One man can't scull two boats."

The navigation to which he devoted all his powers for more than twenty years before his death in 1841 was that of the bark of peace. His boarding it was due in large measure to his reading of Worcester's "Solemn Review" and other tracts with which, through the multiplication of peace societies, the public began to be liberally provided. Signing himself "Philanthropos," he became a bountiful source of contributions to the press and of pamphlets in advocacy of world peace. The pseudonyms of "Philo Pacificus" and "Philanthropos" were themselves characteristic of the time. It was reserved for later champions of the cause to find themselves blessed with names of such eternal fitness as Love, Trueblood, Smiley, and — *per contra* — Gunn. Quite as strictly contemporaneous as Ladd's signature was the tone of much of his writing. Take, for example, a passage in his pamphlet, *On the Duty of Females to Promote the Cause of Peace:* "The distribution of Peace tracts is an employment peculiarly adapted to females. No man of gallantry, or even of common civility, will refuse to read a Peace tract presented by a lady."

Such a fragment, however, is by no means typical of the mass of Ladd's writing. As the first president of the American Peace Society, established in 1828 to bring into coöperation many bodies with a common purpose, and as a Christian so zealous that late in life he secured a preacher's license for the extension of his opportunity to present his cause in churches, he had manifold occasions for serious utterance, and often turned them to serious and impressive account. The production which illustrates most clearly the value of his thoughts is the concluding "Essay on a Congress of Nations, for the Adjustment of International Disputes, and for the Promotion of Universal Peace, without Resort to Arms," in a volume of *Prize Essays on a Congress of Nations*, published in 1840 by the American Peace Society. Two gentlemen of New York had offered a prize of one thousand dollars for the best essay on the subject; many manuscripts were offered, and when no one of them seemed to the judges — John Quincy Adams, Chancellor Kent, and Daniel Webster — so much better than its competitors as to command the award, it was decided to print in a single volume five of the best, "together with a sixth, composed by the President, and containing all the matter relevant to the subject which was elicited by the rejected Essays, with such other remarks as might occur to him."

The forthstanding thing about this essay of William Ladd's is that he could claim for it, apparently with reason, the originality of proposing a Congress of Nations and a Court of Nations, as separate but closely related bodies, "either of which might exist without the other, but they would tend much more to the happiness of mankind if united in one plan, though not in one body." Here, if anywhere, is a clear fore-shadowing of the League of Nations, — though without its sanction of force, — the World Court, and their mutual relation. Prophetic also of recent events is the recorded fate of a petition presented to Congress late in 1837 by the New York Peace Society, the American Peace Society, the Vermont Peace Society, "and many other individuals, the members of no peace society," on behalf of an attempt to institute a general Congress of Nations — a project on which the Massachusetts Legis-lature acted favorably early in 1838. According to William Ladd's account of the reception of this memorial by the House of Representatives, "The Chairman of the Committee of Foreign Affairs manifested a strong inclination to have it *laid on the table*." In that committee's report upon the petition, it was declared that " reforms so funda-mental . . . must follow events, and conform to them; they cannot, by any contrivance of man, be made to precede and control them"; and also that "time is the best reformer in such things." If time has proved a more deliberate reformer than William Ladd, he had his contemporaries to whom it must have seemed even more hopelessly slow.

The complete come-outers of William Ladd's period were impatient of all delays. It was inevitable that the anti-slavery, anti-drink, anti-capital-punishment, anti-everything-as-it-is enthusiasts should ally themselves in time with the anti-war cause. In 1838, several months after the Massachusetts Federal Court gave its backing to this cause, a Peace Convention in Boston broke away from the moorings of the American Peace Society, and adopted a Declaration of Sentiments for a more radical organization, The New England Non-Resistance Society. The Declaration was written by William Lloyd Garrison, and signed by thirty-seven men and women of a reforming temper. Most of their names mean little to-day, but anyone familiar with antislavery history will identify such signers, besides Garrison, as Maria W. Chapman and Edmund Quincy, the spirited come-outer and author whose highly respectable background — his father was then President of Harvard — did not deter him in 1839 from returning to Governor Everett his commission as justice of the peace, on the ground that he could not conscientiously hold office under a government which sanctioned the taking of human life. The gravity of this step, quite typical of the seriousness with which the reformers took their reforms, is reflected in these words from Quincy's letter to the Governor: "I do, therefore, in the presence of Almighty God, and before you, as Chief Magistrate of this Commonwealth, hereby abjure and renounce all allegiance which I may at any time have acknowledged myself at any time to owe to any government of man's institution. And I call upon Heaven and you to witness that I have put away from myself this iniquity forever!"

No consistent signer of the Non-Resistance Declaration could have done otherwise than Quincy, for the document committed its adherents to precisely such action. Were the pacifists of our later, more moderate, day to express themselves so unreservedly as their predecessors of ninety years ago, it is hard — or should one say easy? — to think what would happen to them. Witness one passage from the long Declaration:

We register our testimony, not only against all wars, whether offensive or defensive, but all preparations for war; against every naval ship, every arsenal, every fortification; against the militia system and a standing army; against all military chieftains and soldiers; against all monuments commemorative of victory over a foreign foe,[1] all trophies won in battle, all celebrations in honor of military or naval

[1] William Ladd himself had already objected to the project of a Bunker Hill Monument.

exploits; against all appropriations for the defense of a nation by force and arms, on the part of any legislative body; against every edict of government, requiring of its subjects military service. Hence, we deem it unlawful to bear arms, or to hold a military office.

Ladd's great kindliness and humor probably contributed to the avoidance of recriminating words between the American Peace Society and the New England Non-Resistance Society, for the advocates of peace have by no means escaped quarrels amongst themselves. Could they have shared the vision of a farsighted Psalmist when he wrote: "I labour for peace: but when I speak unto them thereof, they make them ready for battle"?

At this very juncture Garrison described Ladd as "a huge and strange compound of fat, good nature, and benevolence." Much more than that he certainly was, when measured by the effect of his written and spoken words. A eulogist went so far as to predict that "the peacemaker of Minot" would outlive "even the Corsican soldier whose insatiate ambition drank the blood of more than five millions of his fellow men." But prophecy is a pitfall, and Garrison ran all its risks when he exclaimed of the day in 1838 on which the Non-Resistance Declaration was adopted: "Mankind shall hail this 20TH OF SEPTEMBER with more exultation

and gratitude than Americans now do the 4TH OF
JULY. This may now be regarded as solemn bom-
bast; but it is prophetical, and shall not fail to
be fulfilled."

It was a time of high hopes, and the stories of
individual men and women warranted all manner
of expectations. Take, for example, the story of
Elihu Burritt, famed as "the Learned Blacksmith."
It reads like a fairy tale. Born at New Britain,
Connecticut, in 1810, he not only began life as a
blacksmith but continued in this occupation until
he was nearing thirty. But a zeal for knowledge
consumed him, like the coals quickened by the
smithy bellows, and from boyhood he performed
prodigies of mental exercise. At first he trained
his memory through portentous self-imposed tasks
in mental arithmetic. Then he took up the study
of languages, ancient and modern. He began
Greek in New Haven, self-taught, but stimulated
by the academic surroundings. At Worcester,
where he gained access to the treasures of the
American Antiquarian Society, he learned to read
upward of fifty languages with more or less
familiarity. When this achievement became known
he began, in 1841, to appear as "the Learned
Blacksmith" on the lecture platform, the popular
arena of the time, and took also to writing for

publication, especially through a journal of his own, *The Christian Citizen*, devoted in large measure to the cause of peace.

Brought through this cause into relations of friendship with correspondents in England, he paid his first visit to that country in 1846, and remained abroad for more than three years instead of the contemplated three months. These were the years of his life which were of the largest significance in relation to the general theme of this paper. Soon after reaching England he took an active part in organizing a League of Universal Brotherhood, both for the abolition of war and for promoting friendly intercourse between peoples. To this end Burritt threw himself especially into the project for cheaper postage, which was one of the items in the postal reforms instituted by Sir Rowland Hill.

Still more conspicuous was Burritt's participation in a series of peace congresses held in Brussels (1848), Paris (1849), and, after a visit to America, in Frankfort (1850), London (1851), and Manchester (1852). The most brilliant of these was the Paris conference, over which Victor Hugo presided, foretelling the day "when a cannon will be exhibited in public museums, just as an instrument of torture is now, and people will be amazed

WILLIAM LADD

ELIHU BURRITT

NOAH WORCESTER

AMERICAN APOSTLES OF PEACE

that such a thing could ever have been"; predicting also "those two immense groups, the United States of America and the United States of Europe, . . . placed in the presence of each other, extending the hand of fellowship across the ocean." Of the two Channel vessels that brought the English delegation of seven hundred to France, Richard Cobden said that if they had sunk on the passage, all the philanthropic enterprises of the United Kingdom would be stopped for a year.

Burritt figured at this congress as Secretary for the United States, which had a considerable representation of delegates. He spoke, as he had spoken before at Brussels and was to speak again at Frankfort, in eloquent advocacy of the plan for a Congress and High Court of Nations, virtually as outlined by William Ladd, acknowledging, at Frankfort, its designation as an American proposal, but tracing its origin back to the days of antiquity and down through the centuries, and claiming as the contribution of his country to the scheme only the results "from the attention which the friends of peace in the United States have given to its development and advocacy during the last twenty years."

What he could not have said with so much propriety was that in his own person there stood before an assemblage of the highest distinction a product of democratic institutions, one risen from the humble plane of a Yankee blacksmith's apprentice, who must have made any American plan seem capable of fulfillment.

II

Thus far we have stepped barely over the line dividing the second half of the nineteenth century from the first. Nor have we paused long enough on the way even to mention such a classic in the literature of the subject as the address of Charles Sumner before the authorities of Boston, July 4, 1845, on "The True Grandeur of Nations," or to name more than a few of the generous company of those, both poets and men of affairs, whose hearts and minds were set against the "last argument of kings" — that thing, as the Hon. James M. Beck once defined war, which is "more than an evil — it is an indecency." We have glanced indeed chiefly at a few individuals, filled with hopes for a millennial world, and imperfectly aware of the truth which William James, much later, was to express when he wrote, "The war against war is going to be no holiday excursion or camping party."

The second half of the nineteenth century must

have been a discouraging time for the friends of peace. It was ushered in by the European up-heavals of 1848. Then came the Crimean War, our own Civil War, the Franco-Prussian, Russo-Turk-ish, and, to name but two more bringing the period to an end, the Spanish-American and Boer Wars. Altogether it was a sanguinary half-century, however the flow of blood may have been staunched by Florence Nightingale and her pioneer nurses in the Crimea and by the first ministrations of the Red Cross in the Franco-Prussian War. Out of our Civil War, moreover, came a notable forward step in the application of arbitration to points at issue between nations. The United States had serious claims against Great Britain, especially for the depredations of the Confederate vessel Alabama, built and fitted out in England. The Treaty of Washington (1871) provided for a settlement of these matters by arbitration at Geneva. The chosen arbitrators met, and in 1872 reached an agreement which made the Hotel de Ville of Geneva an ideal resting-place for the ploughshare mentioned on an earlier page.

As the century proceeded from the seventies to its close, the sentiment of which the Geneva Award was the expression seemed to be gaining ground in many directions. Before the end of the eighties the Interparliamentary Union, an international body made up of members of the Legislatures of many lands, began its effective work towards promoting the practice of arbitration in differences between nations. Societies already in the field maintained and increased their efforts. Quakers, to be counted on in war and peace to stand by their own guns, continued their support. In 1896 Carl Schurz, who had commanded Union troops in the Civil War, gave voice to a common feeling when he said, in an address before an American Conference on International Arbitration in Washington: "I am confident our strongest, most effective, most trustworthy and infinitely the cheapest coast-defense will consist in Fort Justice, Fort Good-Sense, Fort Self-Respect, Fort Good-Will, and, if international differences really do arise, Fort Arbitration." And in the same speech he met the objection of those who feared that our freedom of action might be hampered when he asked, "What will you think of a man who tells you that he feels himself intolerably hampered in his freedom of action by the Ten Commandments or the criminal code?" Such was the feeling that found an increasingly wide acceptance.

From an unexpected quarter this feeling received

a strong reënforcement throughout the world when in 1898 the Czar of Russia issued his famous Rescript, calling for a meeting of delegates from all governments with representatives accredited to the Imperial Court to consider the maintenance of a general peace and the possible reduction of excessive armaments. It is a curious circumstance that the Czar of Russia, Alexander I, as the leader in the formation of the Holy Alliance of three monarchs in 1815, received in 1817 from the Reverend Noah Worcester all the early publications of the Massachusetts Peace Society, and wrote, in acknowledgment of the gift: "The object which this Philanthropic Institution has in view, the dissemination of the principles of amity and peace among men, meets with my cordial approbation."

The Holy Alliance — announced to the world in the very week in which the Massachusetts Peace Society was formed — fell far short of the hopes of its imperial champion. But the motives which inspired it did not perish; indeed, as inherited motives, they are believed to have actuated quite definitely the Czar Nicholas II in issuing the Rescript which led to the First Hague Conference in 1899. Twenty-six of the governments of the world, including that of the United States, were represented at this gathering. The English journalist,

William T. Stead, in the process of sounding representative men with respect to their feeling towards the objects of the conference, received from Mark Twain a message of characteristic flavor, yet expressing a widespread state of mind: "The Czar is ready to disarm. I am ready to disarm. Collect the others; it should not be much of a task now." Another observation of Mark Twain's had more than a passing significance: "Of course, we cannot expect all of the great powers to be in their right mind at one time." A younger humorist and sage, Mr. Dooley, made note of the fact that with "the powers" summoned to The Hague were joined "manny of the weaknesses."

Of course the task that Mark Twain regarded so blithely proved as far from a "holiday excursion" as William James predicted. Between the First Hague Conference in 1899 and the Second in 1907 the Russo-Japanese War placed the Czar in an ironic position. But to this Second Conference the representatives of forty-four nations repaired, and the conventions adopted at both Conferences constituted a body of international statute law that has served certainly a useful, if not a world-saving, purpose. The convention for international arbitration by means of the Permanent Court at The

Hague is the best known of them all. Under its operations between 1902 and the outbreak of the World War in 1914, fifteen cases, in four of which the United States was involved, were settled by the Court. In the year 1910 the cause of which The Hague had become the centre received a vast support from America through the establishment of the World Peace Foundation, endowed with $1,000,000 by Edwin Ginn of Boston, and of the Carnegie Endowment for International Peace with a fund of $10,000,000. At about the same time Andrew Carnegie made a contribution of $1,500,000 to the erection of the Peace Palace at The Hague.

Mark Twain.

Vienna Jan 9

Dear Mr Stead

The Czar is ready to disarm: I am ready to disarm. Collect the others. it should not be much of a task now **Mark Twain**

Just a century after the formation of the first Peace Society in the world the Third Hague Conference was to have met in 1915. We know all too well what happens to "the best-laid plans of mice and men." In the summer of 1914 the world, ill-prepared by bonfire glows from the Balkans, burst into flames, and the very idea of a Peace Conference before the World War should end became a mockery. The skeptics had indeed some reason to wag their heads and declare, with Roosevelt, that the efforts of the extremists, "all their peace congresses and peace conventions," had "amounted to precisely nothing in advancing the cause of peace."

III

In what remains to be said the name of Woodrow Wilson must occupy a conspicuous place. It is still a name of controversy, a red rag in many pastures. The time has not yet come when all appearance of partisanship can surely be avoided in writing about the efforts of this war-time President of the United States to promote the world organization of peace. But at least one can try to stick to facts and their reasonable interpretation.

Let us begin, then, with the fourteenth of the

Fourteen Points set forth by President Wilson in an address to both Houses of Congress on January 8, 1918, as a programme for the settlement of the World War, and accepted by the antagonists on both sides as the basis of the Armistice of November 11, 1918, and the peace that was to follow. The culminating point read thus:

XIV. A general association must be formed under specific covenants for the purpose of affording mutual guarantees of political independence and territorial integrity to great and small states alike.

President Wilson had good reason to believe that something of this sort represented a general desire on the part of thoughtful Americans. As early as 1910 Theodore Roosevelt, in addressing the Nobel Peace Committee, declared, "It would be a master stroke if those great powers honestly bent on peace would form a league of peace, not only to keep the peace among themselves, but to prevent, by force if necessary, its being broken by others." Again, in 1915 Roosevelt reverted to this topic under the heading, "Utopia or Hell?" and advocated, for the international tribunal he had in view, "the rule that the territorial integrity of each nation was inviolate" — the very rule, embodied in Article X of the League Covenant, which at a later day proved most obnoxious to opponents of the League. It was also in 1915 that Senator Lodge in a commencement address at Union College expressed himself in these terms:

It may seem Utopian at this moment to suggest a union of civilized nations in order to put a controlling force behind the maintenance of peace and international order, but it is through the aspiration for perfection, through the search for Utopias, that the real advances have been made. At all events it is along this path that we must travel if we are to attain in any measure to the end we all desire of peace on earth.

Eight days after Senator Lodge made this address the League to Enforce Peace, on June 17, 1915, was organized in Philadelphia, with the Hon. William H. Taft as its president, and President Lowell of Harvard University as chairman of its executive committee. This organization, with concrete proposals for the formation of an international league when the war should end, did much to concentrate American public opinion in favor of such an enterprise.

All this formulation of opinion antedated any effort of President Wilson's in the direction of a League of Nations. Indeed he was a late comer into the movement. Through the first year and a half of his administration as President he devoted himself to progressive legislation, with substantial results. For more than two years from the outbreak of the War in August, 1914, he bent his energies to the preservation of an official American neutrality, with the object of bringing the force of a great nation outside the conflict into valuable play at its conclusion. When this effort was defeated by the intolerable provocations of the German Government, especially in submarine warfare, Wilson and the great majority of his countrymen were thoroughly at one in entering the war, all the resources of patience having failed, as the quickest and surest path to peace. Many thought we should have entered it sooner, for still quicker and surer settlement. Precisely what would have happened in those conditions must remain conjectural. What did happen is known — that a virtually unanimous country faced the war we were entering at last on the very terms in which Wilson defined it, as a great crusade, gave to the draft law and the loan campaigns the support which ensured their success, and thus turned the tide of battle at the front and contributed an essential element to the final victory. Everything goes to indicate that in Wilson's conception of these events the victory itself would have fallen far short of completeness had it not been used for the realization of his "fourteenth point," the League of Nations, the climax of all the war aims.

To secure this realization he had to fill the place of commander in two battles — the Battle of Paris and the Battle of Washington, the first a hard-won victory, the second a hard-fought defeat. In each of these fights, as in every great battle, the personality of the commander played an important part — what the man was no less than what he did.

It is harder to get at what Wilson was than at what he did. The late Frank I. Cobb, of the *New York World*, declared him "totally deficient in the art of advertising" — a statement explained by the further words: "He was an eloquent pleader for the principles in which he believed, but he had no faculty whatever for projecting himself into the picture." This failure to dramatize his personality has been noted by another observer at close range, Mr. Ray Stannard Baker: "He can express — and no one better anywhere — what he thinks; but not what he did, or why or how."

There need be no surprise therefore that those who admired and trusted him, knowing him well, saw him quite otherwise than those who, knowing him with none of the advantages of intimacy, disliked and distrusted him. These were many,

WOODROW WILSON
PORTRAIT BUST BY R. BRYANT BAKER

and over against them stood the multitude of
those who, knowing him chiefly through his
thoughts and words, winged in peace and war
with the hopes and aspirations of men, irrespective
of place and privilege, counted him the true prophet
of a new day.

A prophet is of a double authority when he is
also the son of a prophet, and Woodrow Wilson
derived his fundamentally religious spirit — like
the quality which the friendly call determination
and the unfriendly obstinacy — from a long line
of Scotch-Irish Presbyterians. His father and his
mother's father were Presbyterian ministers, whose
traits and habits directly moulded his own. He
is reported to have told a story of his father which
might have been told of himself. At a meeting of
ministers who were recounting their religious experiences one of them turned to the Rev. Joseph R.
Wilson, who sat silent, and asked, "Have you no
religious experiences, Dr. Wilson?" "None to
speak of," came the reply. Wilson himself was
conscious of his inherited qualities, as when he
said, at a public luncheon in London: "So far as
I can make out I was expected [on coming to
Europe] to be a perfectly bloodless thinking
machine, whereas I am perfectly aware that I
have in me all the insurgent elements of the human

race. I am sometimes by reason of long Scottish tradition able to keep these instincts in restraint. The stern Covenanter tradition that is behind me sends many an echo down the years."

Besides his inherited traits Wilson brought to his task as President and peacemaker some of the characteristics of a university teacher and executive — the qualities which explained a certain note of derision in the appellation, "Doctor" Wilson. It was also in a London speech that he expressed himself in this regard. Referring to the idea of a League of Nations as something "indulgently considered as the interesting thought of closeted students," he proceeded: "It was thought of as one of those things that it was right to characterize by a name which, as a university man, I have always resented. It was said to be academic, as if that in itself were a condemnation — something that men could think about, but never get. Now we find the practical leading minds of the world determined to get it."

There seems no doubt that ideas did interest him more than persons — at least in so far as he made his thoughts known to the public. A writer in the *New Republic*, analyzing Wilson's work at the Peace Conference, complained of "the invincible abstractness of his mind. To him railroad cars are not railroad cars, but a gray, generalized thing called Transportation; people are not men and women, corporeal, gross, very human beings, but Humanity — Humanity very much in the abstract." On the other hand, look at the account of his affectionate, humorous family life, written by a brother of the first Mrs. Wilson; heed the report of friends and colleagues with respect to his remarkable personal charm in social intercourse; recall the spell of his oratory; and the Covenanter dealing only in abstractions disappears. Even the tales of his reluctance to listen to other opinions than his own are offset by the statement of Mr. Thomas W. Lamont concerning his course in Paris: "I hear it repeated that he was unwilling to take counsel with his delegation. That is untrue. He constantly and earnestly sought the advice of his associates."

On every hand one meets with contradictions about Wilson and the work he did. The verdict of history in this matter must be awaited with such patience — and longevity — as one can command. Meanwhile it is well to keep certain central facts in mind. One of these is that the ideas of which the League of Nations is the embodiment did not at all originate with Woodrow Wilson. Another is that but for him the League would never have come into existence as an element in the Treaty which brought the World War to its end. Just as Theodore Roosevelt was the direct cause of Wilson's election to the presidency, so his enemies — as Colonel House has suggested — have done most, through forcing him into the place of chief sponsor and defender of the League of Nations, to ensure his permanent place among the few Americans who belong to the whole world.

Back of the immediate sentiment aroused during the war in favor of some international endeavor towards permanent peace stood the accumulation of effort which this chapter has sketched. Wilson went to Paris with a tentative draft for a League Covenant based on English and American ideas not originally his own. At Paris these were supplemented by other suggestions, especially from Lord Robert Cecil and General Smuts, and it was three weeks after the Peace Conference opened, on January 12, 1919, that the League Commission of the Conference was presented with drafted proposals as a basis for discussion.

Some day the incidents of the two battles which Wilson fought in Paris and Washington will provide the material for a tragic drama. Enduring tragedy is not concerned with small persons and

small events. If Wilson failed to dramatize himself, the dramatist will find, made to his hand,
the scenes, the very dialogue, of a great and moving
play.

By way of prologue, Woodrow Wilson — who
should not be represented as a demigod but as a
human being with the fallibilities of his kind —
will be seen on the George Washington, sailing
from New York, December 5, 1918, against the
advice of many friends, discredited at home by
the recent defeat of his party at the polls, yet determined to exert all the force of his influence, political
and personal, to accomplish the purposes for
which, in his view, the war had been fought and
won; realizing the heights to which the hopes of
the world had risen, and saying to a friend on deck
one day, "What I seem to see — with all my heart
I hope that I am wrong — is a tragedy of
disappointment."

Then will come a scene revealing the enthusiasm
with which the people, rather than the politicians,
of Europe received him — a municipality renam-
ing a street in his honor, a peasant burning a
candle before his picture, a popular acclaim such
as only an accepted deliverer of mankind could
evoke.

A scene at the Peace Conference might follow.

Let it come near the end of that long conflict, with intimations of broken physical strength, an unavoidable calamity for one who replied to an inquiry about his health, "Very well for one who is fighting all the time. I think I'll be fighting in my sleep if this goes on"; with suggestions of an organized backfire of criticism from America, planned to undermine his influence in Paris; with some appreciation of the significance of the story, whether true or not, that every day on waking up Clemenceau gave himself a Coué-like treatment by saying, "Georges Clemenceau, you *do* believe in the League of Nations." This scene should show the American President yielding with bitter reluctance on certain contested points, preferring half a loaf to no bread, nursing his depleted physical and nervous forces, yet unbeaten in spirit, and comforting himself — it might well have been — with the solace of Ulysses: "Though much is taken, much abides."

There are tragedies in which the climax of dramatic intensity comes too soon. Not so in the drama of Wilson's devotion to the cause he espoused and led. There is still to be depicted a scene from the days of his effort to refer his plea for American participation in the League of Nations from the Senate to the people of the United States.

All warnings that the strain of extended railway travel and frequent speaking throughout the United States would be too much for him went unheeded. Just before the final, inevitable breakdown, in the form of a stroke of paralysis which made this known soldier truly a "war casualty," he said in his last public address, at Pueblo, Colorado, September 25, 1919: "There is one thing American people always rise to and extend their hand to, and that is the truth of justice and of liberty and of peace. We have accepted the truth, and we are going to be led by it, and it is going to lead us, and through us the world, out into pastures of quietness and peace such as the world never dreamed of before."

Nor is this the very end of the drama. The playwright has yet another scene to construct — in the President's sick-room, either in the White House, while the Senate was rejecting the Treaty of Versailles and with it the League of Nations, or in the silences of Woodrow Wilson's retirement to the private life of an invalid, his house the shrine of many pilgrims, its doors opened but to occasional intimate visitors. One of these visitors, Lord Robert — now Viscount — Cecil, has reported finding in him, in 1923, "the same courtesy, calm and dignified, which I had known when I called upon him in his Presidential lodgings in Paris," and manifestly the same spirit, for in answer to the caller's request for counsel regarding his own work for the League, the invalid made reply, "But remember we are winning. Make no concessions." Another visitor, as Wilson's death, on February 3, 1924, drew near, relates a talk with a few friends about the League of Nations. "I am not sorry I broke down," he reports Wilson as saying; and adding, "But as it is coming now, the American people are thinking their way through, and reaching their own decision, and that is the better way for it to come."

Here are but vague suggestions for a few scenes. A wide field for choice lies spread before the dramatist who will appear when the time is ripe for him.

A large portion of this chapter has dealt with peace societies. As long ago as 1920, before Woodrow Wilson retired to private life, President Butler of Columbia made this statement: "We have arrived at a point where a peace society, pure and simple, seems to be an anachronism. The whole world is committed sentimentally and intellectually, except as to what Mr. Roosevelt used to call its lunatic fringes, to a policy of international peace. It is no longer necessary to discuss that question with anybody."

Thus events which only yesterday were called current pass into history. In 1925 the League of Nations, like a child or a convalescent growing constantly steadier on its legs, accomplished directly and indirectly more than ever before in the direction of that European stability with which the peace of the world is so intricately involved. Without entering into detail it is enough to recall, as a single illustration, the treaties of Locarno. In 1926 the United States Senate voted, with certain reservations, — the ultimate consequences of which are still to be seen,—for the adhesion of this government to the Permanent Court of International Justice which came into existence together with the League. The old clamor against even the most casual contact with the institution which its enemies delighted to call "the evil thing with a holy name" had lost its potency. The ensuing fiasco at Geneva gave the enemies of the League a welcome occasion for railing. Yet, at least in America, the political animosities that entered disastrously into a question involving the underlying principles of religion seem surely fading with the passage of time.

Whether changing conditions will by degrees

bring the people of the United States to feel that a League which is serving the rest of the world to advantage may serve them also, whether they will even be moved by what their coöperation might do for it, none but a proved prophet would venture to predict. In the realm of fact the League stands before the world to-day as the realized dream of the centuries, the most promising agency in existence for the diminishing, if not the abolition, of war. It may even be that the words of Maximilian Harden will find their way into the same realm of fact: "Only one conqueror's work will endure — Wilson's thought."

CHIEF SOURCES OF INFORMATION

CHIEF SOURCES OF INFORMATION

THE ensuing lists, to be used as signposts rather than detailed maps, make no pretense to bibliographical completeness. Many books not mentioned here, and many articles listed in the *Readers' Guide to Periodical Literature* but not included below, have been consulted.

I

THE RED CROSS AND CLARA BARTON

Clara Barton: *The Red Cross: a History of This Remarkable International Movement in the Interest of Humanity.* Washington, 1898; *A Story of the Red Cross: Glimpses of Field-work.* New York, 1904; *The Story of My Childhood.* New York, 1907.

William E. Barton: *The Life of Clara Barton, Founder of the American Red Cross.* 2 vols. Boston, 1922.

Percy H. Epler: *The Life of Clara Barton.* New York, 1915.

L. P. Brockett and Mrs. M. C. Vaughan: *Woman's Work in the Civil War.* Philadelphia, 1867.

H. P. Davison: *The American Red Cross in the Great War.* New York, 1919.

Gustave Moynier: *The Red Cross: Its Past and Future* (Tr. by J. Furley). London, 1883.

Mabel Thorp Boardman: *Under the Red Cross Flag at Home and Abroad, with a Foreword by Woodrow Wilson.* Philadelphia, 1915.

George Kennan: *Campaigning in Cuba.* New York, 1899.

L. L. Dock and others: *History of American Nursing.* New York, 1922.

Katharine Prescott Wormeley: *The Cruel Side of War with the Army of the Potomac.* Boston, 1888.

Lytton Strachey: *Eminent Victorians* ("Florence Nightingale"). London, 1918.

Scribner's Magazine, March 1894, "The Sea Island Hurricanes: The Relief," by Joel Chandler Harris.

II

TOLERANCE IN RELIGION — PHILLIPS BROOKS

Phillips Brooks: *Tolerance.* New York, 1887; *Lectures on Preaching.* New York, 1877; *The Influence of Jesus.* New York, 1879; *Essays and Addresses, Religious, Literary, and Social.* New York, 1894; *Letters of Travel.* New York, 1893; Ten volumes of collected sermons, 1878–1904.

Alexander V. G. Allen: *Life of Phillips Brooks.* 2 vols. New York, 1900; *Phillips Brooks, 1835–1893: Memories of His Life, with Extracts from His Letters and Note-Books.* New York, 1907.

William Lawrence: *Phillips Brooks, A Study.* Boston, 1903.

M. A. DeW. Howe: *Phillips Brooks* (in "Beacon Biographies"). Boston, 1899.

Arthur Brooks: *Phillips Brooks* (memorial sermon). New York, 1893.

Thomas M. Clark (Bp.): *The Strong Staff Broken* (memorial sermon). Boston, 1893.

Charles A. L. Richards: *Remembrances of Phillips Brooks by Two of His Friends.* Boston, 1893.

M. C. Ayers: *Phillips Brooks in Boston; Five Years' Editorial Estimates*. Boston, 1893.

Phillips Brooks as His Friends Knew Him (articles from the *Congregationalist*). Boston, 1903.

George F. Seymour, (Bp.): *An Open Letter to the Rt. Rev. W. C. Doane in reference to the Consecration of the Rt. Rev. Dr. Brooks (Bp. of Mass.) by the Bp. of Springfield*. Springfield, 1892.

Lloyd McK. Garrison: *An Illustrated History of the Hasty Pudding Club Theatricals*. Cambridge, 1897.

Charles Carroll Everett: *Sons of the Puritans*. Boston, 1908.

Lyman P. Powell: *Heavenly Heretics*. New York, 1909.

Phillips Brooks; Addresses, with Introduction by Julius H. Ward. Boston, 1893.

Scrapbook of clippings about Phillips Brooks. Boston Public Library.

Phillips Brooks, a Memorial: The United Service of the Churches of Boston at the Old South Meeting-House, January 30, 1893. Boston, 1894.

Henry Caswall: *America and the American Church*. London, 1839.

Sarah Stuart Robbins: *Old Andover Days; Memories of a Puritan Childhood*. Boston, 1908.

Edmund Gosse: *Father and Son; Biographical Recollections*. New York, 1908.

D. C. Weston: *Scenes in a Vestry*, etc. Augusta, Maine, 1841.

Annie Fields: *Life and Letters of Harriet Beecher Stowe*. Boston, 1897.

Robert Baird: *State and Prospects of Religion in America*. New York, 1856; *Progress and Prospects of Christianity in the United States of America*. London, 1851.

The Old South Council Called for Installation of the Rev. George A. Gordon, April 2, 1884. Boston, 1884.

George A. Gordon: *Humanism in New England Theology.* Boston, 1920; *My Education and Religion; an Autobiography.* Boston, 1925.

Theodore T. Munger: *Horace Bushnell, Preacher and Theologian.* Boston, 1899.

III

THE LONG DRIVE FOR TEMPERANCE — FRANCES E. WILLARD

Frances Elizabeth Willard: *Glimpses of Fifty Years; the Autobiography of an American Woman.* Boston, 1889; *Nineteen Beautiful Years, or Sketches of a Girl's Life, with Preface by J. G. Whittier.* New York, 1864; *A Wheel within a Wheel; How I Learned to Ride the Bicycle, with Some Reflections by the Way.* New York, 1895; *How to Win: a Book for Girls.* New York, 1886; *Do Everything: a Handbook for the World's White Ribboners.* Chicago, 1895; *Woman in the Pulpit.* Boston, 1888; *A Classic Town: the Story of Evanston, by an Old-Timer.* Chicago, 1894; *A Great Mother: Sketches of Madam Willard* (with Mrs. Minerva Brace Norton). Chicago, 1894.

Ray Strachey: *Frances Willard, Her Life and Work, with an Introduction by Lady Henry Somerset.* London, 1912.

Gamaliel Bradford: *Portraits of American Women* ("Frances E. Willard"). Boston, 1919.

A Life of Service; Sketches of Frances E. Willard. Chicago, n.d.

R. F. Dibble: *Strenuous Americans* ("Frances E. Willard"). New York, 1923.

William Makepeace Thayer: *Women Who Win; or, Making Things Happen* ("Frances E. Willard"). New York, 1896.

U. S. 58th Congress: *Three Addresses. Statue of F. E. Willard, Erected in Statuary Hall. Proceedings on the Occasion of the Reception and Acceptance of the Statue from the State of Illinois.* U. S. Document 4778, Washington, 1905.

Anna Adams Gordon: *The Beautiful Life of Frances E. Willard.* Chicago, 1898.

Alonzo Potter (Bp): *The Drinking Usages of Society.* Pittsburgh, 1852.

Sir Arthur Newsholme: *Prohibition in America and Its Relation to the Problem of Public Control of Personal Conduct.* London, 1922.

J. Koren: *Alcohol and Society.* New York, 1916.

H. Münsterberg: *Prohibition and Social Psychology.* New York, 1908.

Elizabeth Putnam Gordon: *Women Torch-Bearers: the Story of the Woman's Christian Temperance Union.* Evanston, 1924.

Vance Thompson: *Drink and Be Sober.* New York, 1915.

E. C. Adams and W. D. Foster: *Heroines of Modern Progress.* New York, 1913.

Anna Howard Shaw: *The Story of a Pioneer* (with the collaboration of E. Jordan). New York, 1915.

John B. Gough: *An Autobiography.* Boston, 1845.

Frank J. Mathew: *Father Mathew, His Life and Times.* London, 1890.

Goffiana; a Review of the Life and Writings of John B. Gough, by One Qualified; with the Testimony pro and con, Compared and Weighed. Boston, 1846.

Lyman Beecher: *Autobiography, Correspondence,* etc. 2 vols., ed. by C. Beecher. New York, 1864–65.

Ida Husted Harper: *The Life and Work of Susan B. Anthony.* 3 vols. Indianapolis, 1899–1908.

M. F. Eastman and Mrs. H. C. C. Lewis: *Biography of Dio Lewis*. New York, 1891.

K. Fitzpatrick: *Lady Henry Somerset*. Boston, 1923.

Mrs. M. N. Stanard: *Colonial Virginia, Its People and Customs*. Philadelphia, 1917.

Abraham Lincoln: *Complete Works*, comprising his Speeches, Letters, State Papers, and Miscellaneous Writings, edited by John G. Nicolay and John Hay. New York, 1894.

William E. Barton: *The Life of Abraham Lincoln*. 2 vols. Indianapolis, 1925.

Ervin Chapman: *Latest Light on Abraham Lincoln*. New York, 1917.

Andrew McFarland Davis: "The Law of Adultery and Ignominious Punishments." Worcester, 1895. From *Proceedings of the American Antiquarian Society*, April 24, 1895.

William Root Bliss: *Side Glimpses from the Colonial Meetinghouse*. Boston, 1894.

Andrew Preston Peabody: *Harvard Reminiscences*. Boston, 1888.

Edmund Quincy: "Commencement Day." (In Vaille, F. O., and Clark, H. A., *Harvard Book*, v. 2, 1875.)

John Pierce: "Commencements at Harvard 1803–48." (In *Mass. Hist. Soc. Proc.*, v. 5, 1889–90.)

Many temperance pamphlets in Boston Athenæum.

IV

THE NEW USES OF GREAT WEALTH
THE ROCKEFELLERS

John D. Rockefeller: *Random Reminiscences of Men and Events*. New York, 1909.

John D. Rockefeller, Jr.: *The Personal Relation in Industry*. New York, 1917.

Ida M. Tarbell: *History of the Standard Oil Company*. 2 vols. New York, 1904.

Gilbert Holland Montague: *The Rise and Progress of the Standard Oil Company*. New York, 1903.

Frederick T. Gates: *The Truth about Mr. Rockefeller and the Merritts*. New York, n.d.

Sarah K. Bolton: *Famous Givers and Their Gifts*. New York, 1896.

Edwin Wildman: *Famous Leaders of Industry*. Boston, 1920.

David Allen Robertson: *The Quarter-Centennial Celebration of the University of Chicago*, June 2–6, 1916. Chicago, 1918.

Andrew Carnegie: *The Gospel of Wealth and Other Timely Essays*. New York, 1900.

Carnegie Endowment for International Peace: *A Manual of the Public Benefactions of Andrew Carnegie*. Washington, 1919.

Maximilian Harden: *Monarchs and Men* ("Tolstoi and Rockefeller"). Philadelphia, 1913.

Final Report of the Commission on Industrial Relations, U. S. Senate Document 415, 64th Congress, Washington, 1916.

General Education Board Reports, 1902–14, 1915–

Rockefeller Foundation, Annual Reports, 1913–

Hastings B. Hart: *How to Give Wisely $25,000 to $1,000,000, with Letters of Advice from Leading Authorities*. Russell Sage Foundation, 1921.

American Foundations. Bulletin of the Russell Sage Foundation Library. New York, 1924.

Encyclopædia Britannica: Article on "Charity and Charities."

V

AMERICAN LABOR — SAMUEL GOMPERS

Samuel Gompers: *Seventy Years of Life and Labor — an Autobiography*. New York, 1925; *Labor and the Common Welfare*. New York, 1919; *Labor and the Employer*. New York, 1919; *American Labor and the War*. New York, 1919.

Samuel Gompers and Henry J. Allen: *Debate at Carnegie Hall, N. Y., May 28, 1920*. New York, 1920.

John R. Commons and Others: *History of Labor in the United States*. 2 vols. New York, 1918.

Mary Ritter Beard: *A Short History of the American Labor Movement*. New York, 1920.

Selig Perlman: *History of Trade Unionism in the United States*. New York, 1922.

Robert F. Hoxie: *Trade Unionism in the United States*. New York, 1917.

George Goodnow Groat: *An Introduction to the Study of Organized Labor in America*. New York, 1916.

John Graham Brooks: *Labor's Challenge to the Social Order*. New York, 1920.

John Mitchell: *Organized Labor, Its Problems, Purposes, Ideals*, etc. Philadelphia, 1903.

George E. McNeil (Ed.): *The Labor Movement, the Problem of To-day*. Milwaukee, 1891.

Washington Gladden: *The Labor Question*. Boston, 1911.

Percy Stickney Grant: *Fair Play for the Workers*. New York, 1918.

William Z. Foster: *Bankruptcy of the American Labor Movement*. Chicago, 1922.

Joseph B. Bishop: *Theodore Roosevelt and His Time, Shown in His Letters*. 2 vols. New York, 1920.

Grosvenor B. Clarkson: *Industrial America in the World War.* Boston, 1923.

Edward M. House and Charles Seymour (Eds.): *What Really Happened at Paris.* New York, 1921.

International Journal of Ethics, July 1918: "The Ideals in the American Labor Movement," by J. P. Frey.

Atlantic Monthly, June 1923: "Autobiography of a Labor Leader," by J. H. Maurer.

Atlantic Monthly, March 1925: "What Manner of Man Was Gompers?" by Benjamin Stolberg.

North American Review, March 1925: "The Passing of Gompers and the Future of Organized Labor," by John Spargo.

VI

WOMAN SUFFRAGE — SUSAN B. ANTHONY

Ida Husted Harper: *The Life and Work of Susan B. Anthony.* 3 vols.   Indianapolis, 1899–1908.

Elizabeth Cady Stanton, Susan B. Anthony, and Matilda Joslyn Gage (Eds.): vols. I–IV; Ida Husted Harper (Ed.): vols. V–VI: *The History of Woman Suffrage.*   New York and Rochester, 1881–1922.

Theodore Stanton and Harriet Stanton Blatch (Eds.): *Elizabeth Cady Stanton as Revealed in Her Letters, Diaries, and Reminiscences.*   2 vols.   New York, 1922.

Scott and Nellie M. S. Nearing: *Woman and Social Progress.* New York, 1912.

A. E. Metcalfe: *Woman's Effort, a Chronicle of British Women's Fifty Years' Struggle for Citizenship*, 1865–1914. Oxford, 1917.

Henry St. George Tucker: *Woman's Suffrage by Constitutional Amendment.*   New Haven, 1916.

Thomas Wentworth Higginson: *Cheerful Yesterdays*. Boston, 1898.

Mary Putnam Jacobi: *Common Sense Applied to Woman Suffrage*. New York, 1894.

Encyclopædia Britannica: first edition (1771) and twelfth (1922): Articles on "Woman."

The Nation, February 14, 1920: "Susan B. Anthony," by Fanny Garrison Villard.

VII

THE ROAD UP FROM SLAVERY — BOOKER T. WASHINGTON

Booker T. Washington: *The Future of the American Negro*. Boston, 1899; *Up from Slavery*. New York, 1901; *Working with the Hands*. New York, 1904; *Tuskegee, Its People, Their Ideals and Achievements*. New York, 1905; *Frederick Douglass*. Philadelphia, 1906; *The Story of the Negro; the Rise of the Race from Slavery*. 2 vols. New York, 1909; *My Larger Education*. Garden City, 1911.

Emmett T. Scott and Lyman Beecher Stowe: *Booker T. Washington, Builder of a Civilization*. Garden City, 1916.

B. F. Riley: *The Life and Times of Booker T. Washington*. New York, 1916.

W. E. Burghardt DuBois: *The Souls of Black Folk*. Chicago, 1907; *The Negro in the South* (with B. T. Washington). Philadelphia, 1907.

The Negro Problem. A Series of Articles by Representative American Negroes of To-day (Washington, DuBois, Paul Lawrence Dunbar, and others). New York, 1903.

Atticus G. Haygood: *Our Brothers in Black*. New York, 1881.

Robert Russa Moton: *Finding the Way Out; an Autobiography.* Garden City, 1925.

Negro Year Book 1925–26.

Edith Armstrong Talbot: *Samuel Chapman Armstrong, a Biographical Study.* New York, 1904.

Benjamin G. Brawley: *Your Negro Neighbor.* New York, 1908.

James Hardy Dillard: *Booker T. Washington, a Christian Philosopher:* Founder's Day Address delivered at Tuskegee Institute, April 5, 1925.

Survey, December 4, 1915: "The Spirit of Tuskegee: How Students, Teachers, and Neighbors took Dr. Washington's Death," by Clement Richardson.

The Southern Workman, Hampton Institute Press: Articles in issues from 1902 to 1925, especially "Washington Memorial Number," January, 1916.

VIII

SWORDS, PLOUGHSHARES, AND WOODROW WILSON

Early Reports of Massachusetts and American Peace Societies, 1816– .

The Friend of Peace, 1815 *et seq.; The Non-Resistant*, 1839 *et seq.; The Advocate of Peace*, 1834– ; and other peace journals.

Pamphlets of the World Peace Foundation, Carnegie Endowment for International Peace, "Old South Leaflets," and daily newspapers.

Noah Worcester: *A Solemn Review of the Custom of War*, etc. Cambridge, 1815. (The signature "Philo Pacificus" was introduced in later editions.)

Henry Ware, Jr.: *Memoirs of N. Worcester, with Preface and Notes by S. Worcester.* Boston, 1844.

Lives of Distinguished Shoemakers. Portland, 1849.

John Hemmenway: *The Apostle of Peace. Memoir of William Ladd, with an Introduction by Elihu Burritt.* Boston, 1872.

George C. Beckwith: *Eulogy on William Ladd.* Boston, 1841.

Charles Northend (Ed.): *Elihu Burritt, a Memorial Volume,* etc. New York, 1879.

G. H. Perris: *A Short History of War and Peace.* London, 1911.

Wendell P. and Francis J. Garrison: *William Lloyd Garrison,* 1805–1879; *the Story of His Life.* 4 vols. New York, 1885–1889.

William T. Stead (Ed.): *The War against War, the Journal of the Peace Crusade.* January–March, 1899. London.

Theodore Roosevelt: *America and the World War.* New York, 1915.

Woodrow Wilson. *Why We Are at War.* New York, 1917; *In Our First Year of War.* 1918; *Guarantees of Peace.* 1919; *International Ideals.* 1919.

Edward M. House and Charles Seymour (Eds.): *What Really Happened at Paris; the Story of the Peace Conference by American Delegates.* New York, 1921.

Ray Stannard Baker: *What Wilson Did at Paris.* Garden City, 1919; *Woodrow Wilson and World Settlement, Written from His Unpublished and Personal Material.* 3 vols. Garden City, 1922.

Charles T. Thompson: *The Peace Conference Day by Day; a Presidential Pilgrimage Leading to the Discovery of Europe, with Introductory Letter by E. M. House.* New York, 1920.

Harry Hansen: *The Adventures of the Fourteen Points.* New York, 1919.

Henry J. Ford: *Woodrow Wilson, the Man and His Work, a Biographical Study.* New York, 1916.

Stockton Axson: *The Private Life of President Wilson* (by the brother of his first wife). Boston, 1916.

George Creel: *The War, the World, and Wilson.* New York, 1920.

William E. Dodd: *Woodrow Wilson and His Work.* Garden City, 1920.

Joseph P. Tumulty: *Woodrow Wilson As I Know Him.* Garden City, 1921.

Robert E. Annin: *Woodrow Wilson, a Character Study.* New York, 1924.

Josephus Daniels: *The Life of Woodrow Wilson, 1856–1924.* Chicago, 1924.

William Allen White: *Woodrow Wilson, the Man, His Times, and His Task.* Boston, 1924.

Cobb of the "World," a Leader in Liberalism; Compiled from his Editorial Articles and Public Addresses by J. L. Heaton. New York, 1924.

INDEX